UNIVERSITY OF NORTH CAROLINA
Studies in the Romance Languages and Literatures

NUMBER 32

# NATURAL HISTORY OF THE WEST INDIES

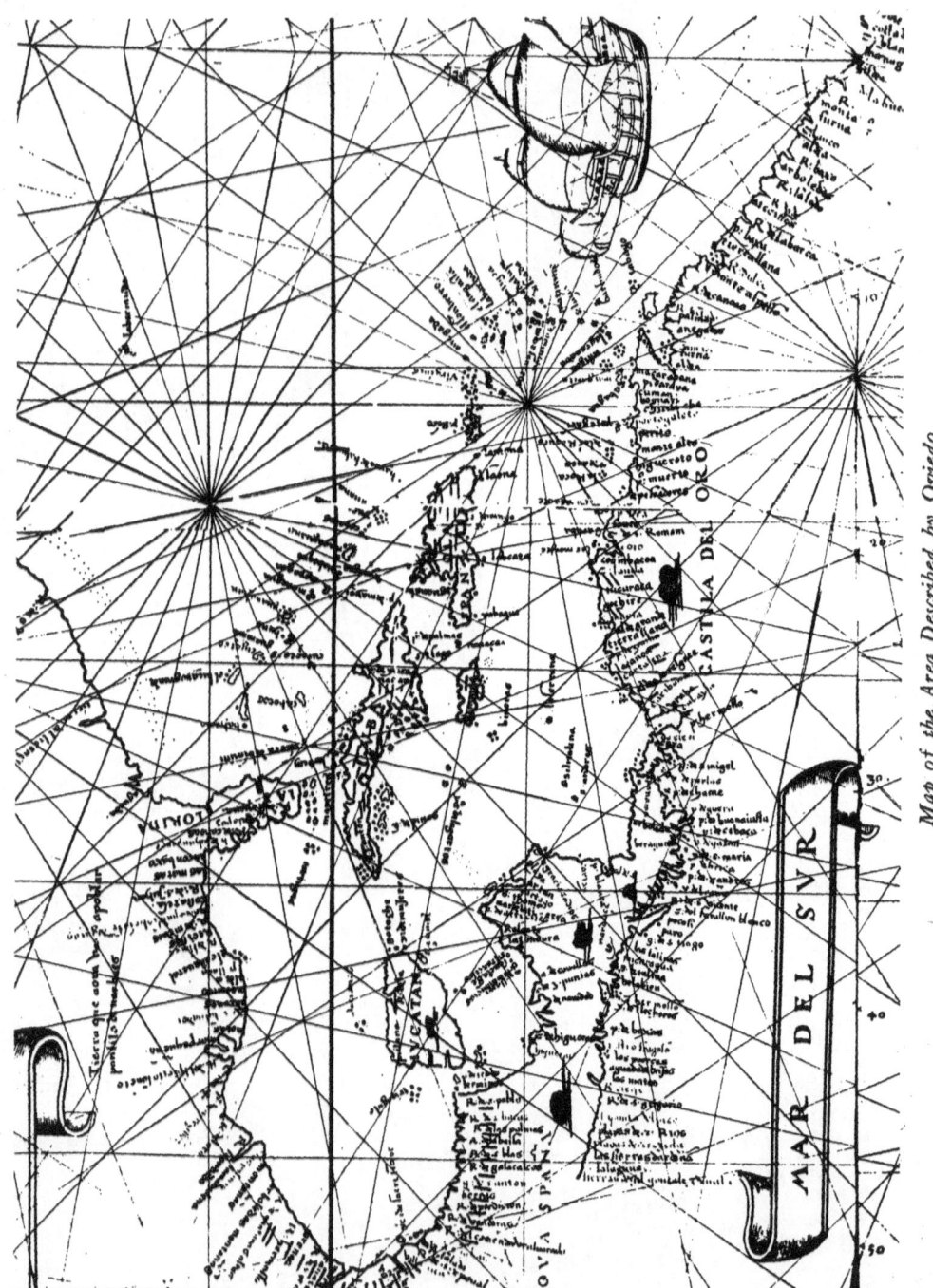

Map of the Area Described by Oviedo

# NATURAL HISTORY OF THE WEST INDIES

By Gonzalo Fernández de Oviedo

Translated and Edited by
STERLING A. STOUDEMIRE

CHAPEL HILL
THE UNIVERSITY OF NORTH CAROLINA PRESS

Copyright 1959 by
The University of North Carolina Press

# FOREWORD

THE TRANSLATOR and editor has felt for a long time that a modern, readable version of Gonzalo Fernández de Oviedo's *Natural History of the West Indies* should be available for the many persons interested in the early history of America who are not able to read Spanish. Oviedo's account appeared in Toledo in 1526, but no complete English version has hitherto been made. A partial but unsatisfactory translation and summary by Richard Eden—*The decades of the new worlde or West India, containing the navigations of the Spaniards*—was published in London in 1555 and was reprinted in 1577. An imperfect reprint of this was published again in London in 1625 by Samuel Purchas—*Hakluytus Posthumus or Purchas His Pilgrimes, Contayning a History of the World in Sea Voyages and Lande Travells by Englishmen and Others*. This version, which was reprinted for the Hakluyt Society in 1902, is fragmentary, inaccurate, unedited, and merged with translations of similar works from the same period.

In describing the strange sights of the New World Fernández de Oviedo shows himself to be a man of keen observation, and readers who cannot find their way through the original will enjoy exploring the islands of the Caribbean and the Panamanian section of the Mainland with him. His *Natural History* should be of interest to the botanist, zoologist, and folklorist, as well as to the amateur historian who may desire to learn something about America before 1607.

Oviedo wrote his *Natural History* in Spanish for the very good reason that he could not have composed it in Latin, if we are to believe Bartolomé de las Casas. Although Oviedo was not a great Latinist, as was Casas, he must have been able to read that language with some facility. The many quotations from his model, Pliny's *Natural History*, almost a century before it was translated into Spanish, indicate that he must have had something more than 'small Latin.' A man of Bartolomé de las Casas' learning would have regarded a halting reading knowledge of Latin as complete ignorance. Even if he had been an expert Latinist, Oviedo would have written only in Spanish, for he argues in several places in his works for the use of the vernacular in the writing of history—that the Spaniard should write in Spanish just as Pliny wrote in Latin and Aristotle wrote in Greek.

But Oviedo's language is not simple and direct, and his style is frequently involved. He was writing at a time when a sentence could go on line after line, adding clause to clause, and the editor has frequently found it difficult to express Oviedo's ideas literally in English. Consequently some paraphrase has been necessary, but in translating, paraphrase is often the surest way to transfer an idea accurately from one language to another.

In many instances the editor has included the scientific names of plants and animals described by Oviedo. In other cases it has been unwise or impossible, because of the haziness of the description, to be specific. This work, however, is not intended for the expert scientist—although he may find here much of interest—but for the general reader.

Preparing this edition has been a labor of love which has been shared by many people. Several of my colleagues in the natural sciences as well as in foreign languages have been of great assistance at many points of the work.

I owe most to Professor Enrique Alvarez López, distinguished Spanish biologist, who personally and through his excellent Spanish edition of the *Historia Natural de las Indias* has cleared up many problems and answered many questions.

The editor is grateful to the Research Council of the University of North Carolina for assistance in the publication of this important document.

Sterling A. Stoudemire

Chapel Hill
March, 1959

# CONTENTS

Editor's Introduction     ix

Oviedo's *Natural History of the West Indies*     1

Glossary of Place Names     123

Bibliography     129

Index     133

# ILLUSTRATIONS

Map of the Area Described by Oviedo — *frontispiece*

Title Page of Oviedo's *Natural History* — 1

Una Hamaca—A Hammock — 42

A Big Tree — 94

Making Fire with Sticks — 95

Leaf of a Banana Tree — 101

### NOTE ON THE ILLUSTRATIONS

The frontispiece shows part of the official Spanish map which was made in 1527 for Emperor Charles V. This map was once believed to be the work of Ferdinand Columbus, who at the age of thirteen accompanied his father on the fourth voyage and who became cartographer at the India House, Seville. Later it was attributed to Nuño García Torreño, but now it is generally believed to be the work of Diego Ribeiro.

The other illustrations are from Oviedo's *Natural History of the West Indies*, which was published in Toledo in 1526.

## EDITOR'S INTRODUCTION

Late in the year 1523, Gonzalo Fernández de Oviedo returned to Spain from the New World. The stormy voyage, which lasted almost two months, was for Oviedo his fourth crossing of the Atlantic, an ocean he was to cross twelve times in his turbulent but distinguished career as the servant of King Ferdinand the Catholic and Emperor Charles V. Oviedo[1] in 1514 had first gone to Spain's western empire as overseer of the mining and smelting of gold for Ferdinand; now he was in the service of Emperor Charles V, Ferdinand's grandson.

Upon his return to Spain in 1523 he immediately went to appeal to the Emperor, whom he did not succeed in seeing until early in 1524 in Vitoria. He made a fervent plea to have Pedrarias Dávila replaced as governor of Castilla del Oro, for this representative of the crown had committed many deeds unworthy of his position as governor; he had already put the popular Vasco Núñez de Balboa to death. In his audience with the Emperor, Oviedo must have mentioned his *General and Natural History of the Indies,* a part of which he had already completed. He had left the manuscript, however, in Santo Domingo. Charles evidently expressed an interest in the narrative, for he wanted to know everything that happened in his vast Empire. Consequently, Oviedo was granted a short leave from his duties in order to write a new history for the Emperor to read in his idle moments—*Natural History of the West Indies*. This history, published in Toledo in 1526, is a brilliant account of the flora, fauna, geography, folklore, and customs of the natives of the Caribbean area, chiefly of the island Hispaniola and the Isthmian area, the section that Oviedo had visited and studied and had come to love. Many bibliographers and historians refer to this work as a 'summary' *(sumario)* of the larger *General and Natural History of the Indies*. In fact, Oviedo in the text refers to the work as a 'summary.' He makes it perfectly clear, however, that it concerns itself principally with the natural and social history of the Indians of Hispaniola and Tierra Firme and not with political history, which is a main theme of his larger work. Perhaps it was

---

1. Gonzalo Fernández de Oviedo is immediately identified when called 'Oviedo.' The correct 'Fernández de Oviedo' is long and unwieldy.

George Ticknor or William Prescott who led later investigators to copy the inaccurate statement that the history published in 1526 is a mere summary of the longer work that had not yet been printed.

Oviedo's eyewitness account of the wonders across the ocean was immediately popular, and had a wide vogue throughout Europe. Many persons derived their principal knowledge of the New World from it, and armchair historians and geographers were quick to incorporate the information in their books on travel and nature. It is said that this is one of the books that influenced Sir Walter Raleigh in his attempts to establish a colony in the New World.

Often Oviedo conveys the impression that he knows he is describing a plant or an animal for the first time; he realizes the importance of his work in world history and consequently goes about his business in a careful, scientific manner. Indeed, he was the first field naturalist to describe accurately many of the wonders of the New World. Here can be found colorful descriptions of many of the plants, animals, and fish that are well known to many Americans today and some of them to people all over the world.

Oviedo was not only interested in describing the natural wonders of the New World; he was also interested in the various American languages he encountered in the provinces and he evidently realized the importance of preserving for posterity the Indian names given to the plants and animals. Oviedo was one of those fortunate souls who appeared at the time to convey to us words from the jungle of Hispaniola or Panama, many of which have come to be international currency: *canoa* (dugout, canoe), *huracán* (hurricane), *maíz* (maize, Indian corn), *cacique, hamaca* (hammock). Others have not found their way into international circulation—such as *churcha* (opossum), *chicha* (corn whiskey), and many others—but they are of interest to the student of languages and have been retained in this text.

Even though Oviedo was a man of little formal schooling and training, he was able to observe the objectivity—at least on many occasions—that is required of a scientist. In many instances he presented the data he was able to gather regarding a particular subject, but refrained from expressing any opinion for the very good reason that he could not formulate one that would satisfy his own curiosity. In that respect Oviedo had a modern point of view and should be set apart from many of his contemporaries who never left their studies but who could produce the answers regarding the whole universe.

The age of discovery and exploration was also the time of the popularity of the Romances of Chivalry. One can easily see how the Spanish reading public would accept the many interesting accounts of Spaniards in the New World. These books took on a fictional aspect, since they were read along with the Romances, and it may not be too much of an exaggeration to say that the Romances themselves took on a quality of truth for the very reason that they were read along side the histories of newly-discovered and far away lands. We should not forget the comment of the innkeeper in *Don Quijote*, who insisted that everything written in the Romances was true and not feigned. Consequently, the histories of Oviedo and much better-known conquistadores served two purposes: they added to the enjoyment of those who devoured the Romances, and they added to the knowledge of those who wanted to study the world.

### LIFE OF OVIEDO

Gonzalo Fernández de Oviedo[2] was born in Madrid in 1478. His father's name is not known, but he may have been Juan de Oviedo, secretary to Henry IV. As a young man Oviedo entered the service of Alphonso of Aragon, second Duke of Villahermosa, nephew of Ferdinand the Catholic. Villahermosa was very fond of young Oviedo and undertook to supervise his military and courtly education. When Oviedo was thirteen years old he was introduced by his sponsor to the Court of the Catholic Sovereigns, then at the peak of its glory, and shortly afterwards he was appointed aid to Prince John. In 1490 he met Columbus, who was at that time only a poor and disillusioned mariner. He also knew Columbus' sons and came to be quite friendly with them and the members of the Pinzón family.

In 1493 Columbus was making preparations for his second voyage and several of Oviedo's friends had already been signed as members of the crew. Displaying as a young man the cu-

---

2. Oviedo has scattered his autobiography throughout his works. The best secondary information on his life is to be found in the magnificent edition of *Historia general y natural de las Indias, Islas y Tierra Firme del Mar Océano*, edited by Amador de los Ríos.

riosity concerning men and places that was to serve him so well in his later travels, Oviedo earnestly requested these acquaintances to observe everything with close scrutiny and to bring him a detailed report of what they saw. At that time he also met Nicolás de Ovando, who was later (1502) to become governor of Hispaniola. Oviedo must have been popular at court for in 1496 Prince John requested that Oviedo be made his Chamberlain. This close friendship of prince and subject came to an abrupt end when Prince John died, October 4, 1497. Overcome by grief, Oviedo decided to leave Spain to seek solace in other lands.

Oviedo spent almost two years in Italy, studying painting, buying books, and talking with young Italians with whom he had common interests, among whom were Jacopo Sannazaro and Pontano. He also served in the army in Sicily, where he met Gonzalo Fernández de Córdoba, the Great Captain. Upon his return to Spain he entered the service of the ill-starred Princess Joanna the Mad. It was at that time that he met Margarita de Vergara, one of the real beauties of her day, whom he soon married, when he was not quite twenty-four years old. His happiness was short-lived, however, for Margarita died in childbirth ten months after her wedding. Once more Oviedo attempted to flee from his emotional blows by leaving the court. On this occasion he went into the army (1503) and fought against the French. The death of Queen Isabella in 1504, worshipped and adored by all her subjects, was a still further sorrow in Oviedo's unhappy youth.

Ferdinand, who had been deeply impressed by the sincerity and studious habits of the young man who had served both his son and his daughter, in 1506 asked Oviedo to write a genealogical history of the rulers of Spain. It was also about this time that Oviedo remarried. A son was born in 1509. For several years Oviedo lived in comparative quiet and happiness, but always dreaming of the possibility of visiting the New World. He could never have guessed just how much of the last fifty years of his life would be spent in that part of the Spanish Empire.

In 1513 the expedition of Pedrarias Dávila was organized and Oviedo was appointed supervisor of the smelting of gold of Tierra Firme, an important post he was to hold until 1532. The expedition of twenty ships sailed from San Lúcar de Barrameda on April 11, 1514. (At this time Oviedo was almost thirty-six years old.) After a voyage of nine days the fleet put in at Gomera, Canary Islands, where it remained for twenty days taking on provisions and having repairs made. The fleet reached Dominica on June 3 and continued on to Santa Marta, the administrative seat of Castilla del Oro, where it arrived on June 12. By June 30 the company had gone on to the city of Santa María del Antigua on the Gulf of Urabá, where they were welcomed by Vasco Núñez de Balboa. Pedrarias Dávila, obeying the King's orders, took over as Governor and immediately proved to be an unbending despot.

In a short time Pedrarias had everything in such turmoil that, under the pretext of taking the King his share of the gold, Oviedo decided to return to Spain to give the monarch a full account of the sad state of affairs in Tierra Firme. Oviedo left Santa María in October of 1515, stopping over at Santo Domingo to pick up the King's gold. Evidently Pedrarias did not have complete confidence in Oviedo, for he sent a bishop and a captain to keep an eye on him and on the gold. Oviedo, however, managed to miss sailing with the fleet and took a later ship which required seventy-five days to reach the Madeira Islands. Often all hands thought they would perish in the mountainous seas.

He arrived at Sevilla in December and immediately went on to Placencia to make his report to King Ferdinand. The monarch must have been well pleased with Oviedo's efforts for he granted him permission to return to Madrid to spend a vacation with his family. Ferdinand lived only a few months after that—he died on January 23, 1517. Oviedo was afraid that the new king, Charles I, later to be the great Emperor Charles V, was not cognizant of the situation in the New World, and so he decided to go to Flanders to make the same report he had made previously to Ferdinand. After a long delay caused by illness and later by shipwreck, Oviedo reached Brussels in August. He was cordially received by Charles, who listened to his story and gave him a handsome financial reward for his services. Oviedo then returned to his family in Madrid and decided to forget the New World. He settled down to a less dangerous and more comfortable existence, and wrote a novel of chivalry, *Don Claribalte,* which was published in 1519 in Valencia.

In September, 1517, Charles V came to Spain, where he granted Diego Columbus the full rights and privileges which had been stripped from his famous father. Oviedo sensed a change of policy for the New World and could not then force himself to remain in retirement. Early in 1518 he was again at court, but he did not succeed in seeing the King until the following year in Barcelona. It was most unfortunate that Bartolomé de las Casas should have been there at the same time. These men, who had such conflicting views regarding the natives of the New World, permitted those views to color their opinions regarding each other. Casas argued to the King that the Indians were mild and docile, that they never should be treated harshly, that they should be converted to the Christian religion. Oviedo was much more realistic: he argued that some of the Indians were docile and friendly but others were fierce, warlike cannibals, and it would be a waste of time and effort to try to convert such savages. Casas won, as he usually did in such disputes.

Even though Charles agreed with Casas in his attitude toward the natives, he still saw in Oviedo a capable and honest servant. Consequently, late in 1519 he appointed him permanent councilman of Nuestra Señora del Antigua and clerk of the court for the whole province, as well as to several other offices. He also commissioned Oviedo to write the official history of the New World. It was at this time that news arrived that Pedrarias Dávila had put to death the popular and able Vasco Núñez de Balboa.

Oviedo returned to Madrid to get his wife and two sons and then made his way to Sevilla, from where the fleet sailed in April. On this voyage the ships put in at Gran Canaria and then proceeded to San Juan, arriving there on June 24, 1520. Oviedo went on to Darién and immediately found that it was almost impossible to come to any kind of agreement with Pedrarias. (It was at this time that Oviedo's eight-year-old son died.) Pedrarias, not wanting the city of Santa María del Antigua to prosper, had moved the seat of the government to Panama before Oviedo had returned from Spain. As a councilman, Oviedo was determined that his city should grow and wax strong, but it was a futile fight. Gradually Spaniards began to leave Santa María in order to go to Panama. Now that the gold was to be carried to Panama, Pedrarias ordered

Oviedo to come there to perform his duty as overseer of the smelting. In August, 1521, Oviedo went to Panama and collected the share of the gold that belonged to the crown, about one-fifth of the total amount. He also upbraided Pedrarias for his efforts to sabotage the city of Santa María del Antigua.

Shortly after Oviedo's return to Darién in November, 1521, his wife died. He hid his grief in furious activity, developing the city, establishing trade agreements with the natives. Evildoers and criminals all fled to Panama, where they were pardoned by Pedrarias. In the course of time all the rough and tough elements of the isthmian area came to hate Oviedo, for he stood for honesty, fair dealing, and good government. He succeeded in putting down several attempts to overthrow him, but he was not able to keep entirely out of danger. On one occasion he was stabbed by a would-be assassin and it was believed that he would certainly die, but almost miraculously he recovered. After three years of bickering and quarreling with Pedrarias, Oviedo was weary. Despairing of being able to agree with the governor, he decided to appeal to the Royal Council of the Indies, and sailed from Darién on July 3, 1523. During these last years Oviedo had written a great deal, especially on his large general history of the Indies.

At the time of his departure Oviedo was seriously ill, and the stormy passage did not help matters. Upon reaching Santiago, Cuba, he was well received by Diego Velázquez, in whose house he remained for two weeks. Velázquez asked him to carry to Charles V news of Juan de Grijalva's discovery of Yucatán. Oviedo then went to Hispaniola, where he found Diego Columbus preparing to sail for Spain, and he asked permission to accompany him. After seeing his wife and children comfortably established in Santo Domingo—he had married again—he sailed for Spain on September 16, 1523. After another tempestuous voyage the travelers reached San Lúcar on November 5.

Oviedo immediately went to request an audience with Charles, which was finally granted him in Vitoria early in 1524. Once more the supervisor of mining poured out his complaints to the Emperor and requested that a governor be sent to replace Pedrarias Dávila. In March, having followed the Emperor to Burgos, Oviedo was fined for not delivering to Pedrarias the gold mined in Darién. After this setback

Oviedo again settled down to a short period of quiet, which he devoted almost entirely to writing. It was in this interlude that he wrote the *Natural History of the West Indies*. In April, 1525 came the news of the capture of Francis I at the battle of Pavia, and almost immediately further news that Pedro de los Ríos had been appointed governor of Castilla del Oro. Oviedo could not contain his joy, and he came out of his semi-retirement to sail to his old fighting grounds with the new governor.

They left Spain on April 30, 1526 and reached Nombre de Dios on July 30. Two years before, Pedrarias Dávila had gone to Santa María del Antigua and had forced all Spaniards to evacuate the city. As soon as the Christians had gone, the Indians took over and burned the city to the ground, and within a few years the jungle had erased all traces of the settlement which was once the foremost outpost of Spain in America, the first city of the mainland.

In 1530 Oviedo was in Hispaniola visiting his wife and children, whom he had not seen for seven years. But his visit was short, for in December of that year he once more sailed for Spain. In 1532, during this visit, Charles V appointed Oviedo's son to the position of checking the gold production, a position that Oviedo himself had held for many years. Oviedo was at the same time appointed official chronicler of the Indies so that he might live more comfortably and remain with his family. He returned to Santo Domingo in the autumn of 1532 and for two years stuck rather closely to his writing. In 1534 he is to be found again in Spain, complaining as was his custom. The primary purpose of this trip was the publishing of his *General and Natural History of the Indies*. In 1535 the first part of the long history came from the press of Juan Cromberger in Sevilla. It had a very warm reception all over Europe, and translations soon appeared in almost every European language. His mission accomplished, Oviedo returned to the New World, arriving at Santo Domingo on January 11, 1536. In November of that year his son who had taken his position, Francisco Fernández de Valdés, was drowned; another child five years of age died shortly afterwards.

In 1541 Part Two of the *General History* was ready for the press but Oviedo was unable to get to Spain until 1546. Even then he could not obtain the necessary permits to have his work published. In all likelihood it was Bartolomé de las Casas who saw to it that the history, in conflict with his own views, was not licensed for publication. In 1549 Oviedo returned to Santo Domingo, where he once more devoted most of his time to writing. He returned to Spain in 1556 and found that the great Emperor for whom he had labored for almost forty years had abdicated and had retired to Yuste. Oviedo, now an old man, felt that it would be futile to try to learn the desires of a new prince, and so devoted his time to the preparation of his manuscripts for the press. He did not live, however, to see the second part of his *General and Natural History* in print (Valladolid, 1557), for he died in the summer of 1557 in Valladolid at the age of seventy-nine, hale and vigorous almost to the last. It is doubtful if Charles V, for whom the account was written, ever saw a copy of Part Two.

Oviedo was definitely a man of action; he fought in Italy and in Sicily, traveled over most of Europe, fought the natives and explored the jungles of the New World, crossed the Atlantic twelve times, served the crown for well over half a century and still found time to write thousands of pages in a wide variety of genres. Among these is the *Natural History of the West Indies,* one of the most fascinating books of the age of exploration.

Oviedo had complete and lasting faith in God, deep respect and reverence for the Emperor, and he was one of the few men in the early sixteenth century who could envision the great importance that one day would be the role of the New World. In all ways—as courtier, as soldier, as historian, as governor, as novelist, as scientist—Oviedo is a shining example of the Renaissance Gentleman.

Uiedo dela natural hystoria delas Indias.
Con preuilegio dela
S.C.C.M.

A summary of the natural and general history of the West Indies, written by Gonzalo Fernández de Oviedo, alias de Valdés, native of the city of Madrid, citizen and councilman of the city of Santa María del Antigua of Darién, in Tierra Firme, giving an account to his Sacred, Catholic, Imperial, Majesty, the Emperor Charles, our Lord, of various things that the said author saw and that are to be found in the West Indies.

This document has been seen and examined in the Royal Council of the Indies and his Majesty has ordered that it be printed so that these great, marvelous, and new things may become well-known to all men; and that no other person can print it or sell it or take it out of these kingdoms except the said Gonzalo Fernández, or someone who has his official permission, under serious penalty, as is stated in detail in the royal privilege that his Majesty has granted.

INTRODUCTION

Prologue and introduction of the said author: addressing this work to his Sacred, Catholic, Imperial, Royal Majesty, the Emperor Charles, the fifth of that name. King of the Spains and of the two Sicilies, on this side of and beyond Faro, and also of Jerusalem and Hungary, Duke of Burgundy, Count of Flanders, and so on, our Lord.

\* \* \* \* \*

Oh Sacred, Catholic, Imperial, Royal Majesty: The wonders of nature are best preserved and kept in the memory of man by histories and books in which they are written by intelligent persons who have traveled over the world and who have observed at first hand the things they describe and who describe what they have observed and understood of such things. This was the opinion of Pliny, the foremost of all natural historians, who wrote a history in thirty-seven books for the Emperor Domitian.[1] A very accurate scholar, Pliny always cited his source when he quoted a story which he had heard or read. He also included in this history many things which he had observed at first hand. In the manner of Pliny, then, in this short study I want to describe for your Majesty what I have seen in your Occidental Empire of the West Indies, Islands and Tierra Firme of the Ocean Sea. Twelve years ago I went to the New World to be overseer of the smelting of gold for your Majesty's grandfather, the Catholic Sovereign, King Ferdinand V, God rest his soul. Since his death I have continued to serve your Majesty in the New World and I hope to continue to do so as long as I shall live.

I have already written much more fully of these and many other things. These accounts are in the papers and chronicles I have been engaged in writing from the time I was old enough to become interested in such affairs. These writings are concerned with what has happened in Spain from 1490 up to now, as well as affairs in other lands and kingdoms where I have traveled. My writings treat the lives of the Catholic Sovereigns, Ferdinand and Isabella, of glorious mem-

---

1. The 1526 edition reads 'Domiciano.' It should have read 'Vespaciano,' for Domitian did not become emperor until 81, two years after the death of Pliny.

ory, up to the end of their days, as well as things that have happened since the accession of your Majesty.

In addition, I have written in separate form[2] all that I have been able to observe and study of the Indies. The document is in the city of Santo Domingo, of the island of Hispaniola,[3] where I have my home and residence and where my wife and children reside. I did not bring these papers here to Spain with me and consequently I am writing this account from memory. In this book I desire to give your Majesty a little pleasure and to summarize certain things regarding the West Indies. Even though these things may have been written about already and eyewitnesses may have described them, they probably are not so accurate as you will find them here. Those who have gone to the Indies on business or for other reasons may have spoken accurately about some or all of these things. Most men, however, would be inclined to forget the details since they have observed those wonders in a casual manner. I, on the other hand, by natural inclination have had keen desire to learn of these things and I have therefore observed them very carefully.

This *Summary* will not reduce the value, as I have said, of the more extensive document which I have already written. Its main purpose I have indicated and as soon as God may return me to my home I shall send you the longer and more complete history.

At the beginning of this account I write thus: As everyone knows, Christopher Columbus, the first Admiral of the Indies, discovered the New World in the time of the Catholic Sovereigns, Ferdinand and Isabella, your Majesty's grandparents, in the year 1491, and returned to Barcelona in 1492 with the first Indians, specimens of the riches, and information of this Occidental Empire. This feat is one of the greatest that any subject ever performed for his Prince, and it is as useful to the realm as it is famous. I say that it is useful because, to be honest, I do not consider the man who is unaware of this a good Castilian or a good Spaniard. Since I have written about this in detail in another place, I do not wish to repeat

---

2. *Historia general y natural de las Indias*, Sevilla, 1535. *Libro XX* de la segunda parte, Sevilla, 1557. Modern eds. Amador de los Ríos, 4 vols., Madrid, 1851-55; in 14 vols., Asunción del Paraguay, 1944-45.
3. The island (now Haiti and the Dominican Republic) was originally given the name Española, 'the Spanish Isle,' and the name we prefer. However, we yield to tradition and here call it Hispaniola.

myself here. I only want to describe a few of the many thousands of things that could be described.

First, I shall deal with the course and the voyage to the New World. Then I shall describe the people who live in that land, and then the animals, birds, rivers, streams, seas, fishes, plants, herbs, things produced by the land, and certain rites and ceremonies of those uncultivated people.

Since I am in haste to return to the Indies to serve your Majesty there, I beg of your Majesty to pardon any lack of order or arrangement that may be found in this book, for indeed it may be less orderly than the larger work I have written. But I should like you to observe the new things in it, for this has been my chief purpose. I write this accurately, as could many trustworthy witnesses who have been to the New World and who have now returned to Spain. There are also others in your Majesty's court, who ordinarily live in the New World, who could write about these things.

1

## THE VOYAGE

The customary course from Spain to the West Indies begins at Sevilla, the location of your Majesty's Board of Trade [India House] and its officials. There the captains and first officers of the ships receive their clearance papers and then embark at San Lúcar de Barrameda, where the Guadalquivir flows into the Atlantic. From there they steer for the Canary Islands, and usually put in at one of two of the seven, which are Gran Canaria or Gomera. There the ships take on fresh supplies of water, wood, cheese, fresh meat, and other things that the masters think should be added to the original provisions brought from Spain. The voyage from Spain to these islands, a distance of about two hundred and fifty leagues, requires approximately a week. From these islands the ships, continuing the voyage, sail about twenty-five days before they sight the headlands of the islands which are reached before they come to the one named Hispaniola. The land that in most instances is first sighted is one of the following islands: Todos Santos [Iles des Saintes], Marigalante [Marie-Galante], Deseada [Désirade], Matitino [Martinique], Dominica, Guadalupe [Guadeloupe], San Cristóbal [Saint Kitts], etc., or one of the many others in that group. Sometimes it so happens that the ships pass without sighting any of these islands, or any others in that vicinity, until they reach the islands of San Juan [Puerto Rico], Hispaniola, Jamaica, or Cuba, which are farther on, or perhaps none of those until they come to Tierra Firme. Such happens when the mate is not skilled in navigation. Yet in making this voyage with skilled seamen, and there are many, one always sights one of those islands first mentioned above. The distance from the Canaries to these Islands is approximately nine hundred leagues. From there to the city of Santo Domingo, which is on the island Hispaniola, the distance is one hundred and fifty leagues. Thus from Spain to that point it is thirteen hundred leagues. Since the ships are usually manned by expert navigators, the voyage is about fifteen hundred leagues. The average voyage may be made in thirty-five or forty days, while the return trip to

Spain requires a longer time, usually about fifty days. However, in this present year of 1525, four ships made the crossing from Santo Domingo to San Lúcar in twenty-five days. But, as we have said, we should not judge by the rare extreme, but by the average.

The voyage is very safe and uneventful over this route to Santo Domingo. From there the ships cross to Tierra Firme in five, six, or seven days, or more, according to their destination, for Tierra Firme is very large and there are different routes and courses we can follow. But the land that is nearest the island Hispaniola and opposite Santo Domingo is five days away. It is better to leave this matter to navigation charts and to the new cosmography, which was not known to Ptolemy and the ancients, who said nothing about it. But since this is not necessary here, I shall go on to other particulars on which I shall dwell at more length than on these matters, which are more appropriate to my *General History of the Indies* than to this present document.

## 2
## THE ISLAND HISPANIOLA

Hispaniola, from Higuey Point to Cape Tiburón is more than one hundred and fifty leagues in length. From the coast of Navidad on the north to Cape Lobos on the south, the island is fifty leagues wide. The city of Santo Domingo is in the southern part of the island at about nineteen degrees north latitude. There are many beautiful rivers and streams on the island and some are quite large, such as the Ozama river which empties into the ocean at Santo Domingo. Other rivers are the Neyba, which flows close by the town of San Juan de la Maguana, the Artibonito, the Haina, the Nizao, and many smaller ones which I do not care to mention. On the island there is a lake [Lake Enriquillo] about two leagues inland, near the town of Yaguana, which extends fifteen leagues or more to the east. In some places it reaches a width of one to three leagues, but for the most part it is considerably narrower. Most of the lake is salty, but where rivers and springs flow into it the water is fresh. The truth is that this lake is really a 'sea eye,' which is very near the sea and contains many different kinds of fish, especially large sharks, that enter the lake from the sea by coming under the land or through a place or places through which the sea flows and forms the lake. This is the opinion of most of those who have seen this lake.

At the time of the discovery, Hispaniola was populated by Indians and was ruled by two great kings, Caonabo and Guarionex, and afterwards it passed to the rule of Anacoana. I do not wish to dwell on the conquest or the cause of the reduction in numbers of the Indians, and thus go about describing things I have described in detail elsewhere. This is not the subject I am to treat here, but other details that your Majesty may not know so well or may have forgotten. Concerning this island, however, I wish to say that there are very few Indians there now, and not so many Christians as there should be, since many of those who once were on the island have gone to other islands or to Tierra Firme. Being men fond of adventure, those who go to the Indies for the most part are unmarried and therefore do not feel obligated to reside in any one place. Since new lands have been discovered and are being discovered every day, those men believe that they will swell their purses more quickly in new territory. Even though some may have been successful in this, most have been disillusioned, especially those who already have established homes and residences in Hispaniola.

I believe beyond any doubt, and this opinion is held by many, that if a prince had no realm except this island, in a short time it would not be inferior to Sicily or England, nor at present is there any reason why either of those islands should be envied. Hispaniola is so rich in natural resources that she could enrich many provinces and kingdoms. In addition to having more rich mines and better gold than have yet been discovered in such quantity anywhere in the world, so much cotton[1] grows wild that if it were cultivated and cared for it would become the best and the most productive in the whole world. There are so many excellent drumstick trees[2] that large quantities of the pods are already being brought to Spain and from Spain they are carried and distributed to many parts of the world. This is increasing so rapidly that it

---

1. *Gossipium barbadense.*
2. *Cañafistula*, the drumstick tree *(Cassia fistula)* an East Indian leguminous tree brought by the Spaniards to the New World. The juice of the seed of the pods was widely used in medicine as a mild laxative.

is really a marvel. On that island there are many rich sugar plantations.³ The sugar is of very good quality and ships loaded with it come to Spain every year.

Plants native to Spain that have been transplanted and cultivated there grow better and in larger quantity than in any part of Europe. They grow and multiply in spite of the fact that they are neglected and not well cared for. The men want the time they would employ in agriculture for other gains and enterprises that more rapidly swell the wealth of covetous souls who have no desire to work. For this reason the settlers do not occupy themselves with growing grain or setting out vineyards, for in the time necessary for these to produce fruit, these products can be had at good prices, for ships carry them there from Spain. In mining, trading, pearl fishing, or in other pursuits, the colonists become wealthy more quickly than they would by sowing wheat or planting vines, as I have said. Some, however, especially those who expect to remain in that land, are engaged in agriculture. There are also many fruits native to Hispaniola, and those that have been carried there from Spain and planted have grown remarkably well.

Farther on I shall describe in detail those things that had their origins on that island and in other parts of the Indies, which have been found there by the Christians. Of the things which have been carried from Spain there can be found on that island, throughout the year, many good vegetables, many fine cattle, sweet orange and bitter orange trees, and very beautiful lemon and citron trees, and these fruits are to be found in abundance. There are many figs throughout the year, many date palms and other plants and trees that have been carried there from Spain.

In Hispaniola there was no quadruped except two species of very small animals that are called *hutía*⁴ and *corí*,⁵ which are very much like rabbits. All other quadrupeds that are there now have been carried from Spain. Consequently it

---

3. Sugar cane was also introduced into the West Indies from the Canary Islands early in the sixteenth century, and came to be a flourishing industry within a few years.
4. *Capromys oedium*.
5. *Cavia cobaya*. For a discussion of the *hutía* and *corí* see Gonzalo Fernández de Oviedo, *De la natural historia de las Indias*, con un estudio preliminar y notas por Enrique Alvarez López, p. 199; also Enrique Fernández López, "Apuntes acerca de los mamíferos americanos conocidos por Fernández de Oviedo," Associação Portuguesa para o Progresso das Ciências, *Ciências Naturais*, Tomo, V, 4a Secção, 445-51.

seems to me unnecessary to speak of them, nor is it necessary to say more than that the cattle as well as other animals have multiplied greatly. Cows have multiplied at such a rate that many cattle kings have more than a thousand or two thousand head, and there are quite a number who have up to three or four thousand head. An occasional herd may have more than eight thousand head. Herds of five hundred or more are quite common. The truth is that the land furnishes some of the best pasturage, clear water, and one of the most temperate climates in the world for such cattle. Consequently the animals are larger and more handsome than those in Spain; and since the weather is mild, and not cold, the cattle are never lean and of bad flavor. Likewise, there are many sheep and swine, and many of the swine and cattle have become wild. Large numbers of dogs and cats that were carried there from Spain for the use of the settlers have escaped to the forests and have become quite vicious, especially the dogs, and they eat the cattle because of the carelessness of the shepherds, who guard the flocks poorly. There are many mares and horses and all the other domestic animals that have been bred from original stock carried from Spain.

There are a number of small towns on this island, concerning which I desire to say only that they are so located that in time they will grow and become famous, because of the fertility and the abundance of the land. Concerning Santo Domingo, the principal city, I wish to point out that with regard to the buildings, no town in Spain—unless it is Barcelona, which I have seen many times—is superior in general. The houses in Santo Domingo are for the most part of stone like those in Barcelona, and the walls are strong and beautiful, constructed of wonderful masonry. The general layout of the city is much better that that of Barcelona, because the many streets are more level and wide and incomparably straighter. Since the city was founded in our own time, there was opportunity to plan the whole thing from the beginning. It was laid out with ruler and compass, with all the streets being carefully measured. Because of this, Santo Domingo is better planned than any town I have seen.

The city is so near the sea that on one side there is only space for the street, which is about fifty paces at the widest point. On one side the waves beat upon live rock and a rugged coast, while on the other side, near the houses, flows the Ozama river, which forms a marvelous port. The ships anchor there near the shore, under the very windows of the houses and no farther from the mouth of the river than the distance from the foot of Monjuich mountain to the monastery of Saint Francis or to the Exchange of Barcelona. In this area the fortress and castle are located, beneath which, and about twenty paces away, the ships pass in order to anchor somewhat further up the river. From the time the ships enter the river until they drop anchor they are never more than thirty or forty paces away from the houses of the city, for on that side the city extends to the edge of the water. One could not find such a beautiful port or river mouth anywhere in the world.

There must be some seven hundred citizens in this city, living in such houses as I have already described. Some of the private homes are so luxurious that any grandee in Spain would find himself most comfortable there. Admiral Diego Columbus, your Majesty's Viceroy, has such a magnificent house that I cannot remember one in Spain a quarter as good. It is well constructed of stone and located on the port. It has many fine rooms and commands a beautiful view of both land and sea. The rooms to be added later will harmonize with the part already constructed. Here your Majesty would be as comfortably lodged as in one of the finest houses in Castile.

A cathedral is now being constructed, and the Bishop and other dignitaries and canons are well provided for. Since there is an abundance of materials and labor, it should be completed soon. From what I have already seen, I believe it will be a magnificent building of good proportions.

There are also three monasteries (Dominican, Franciscan, and Saint Mary of Mercy) which have handsome but modest buildings which are not so grotesque as some of those in Spain. But speaking without prejudice toward any religious order, your Majesty may rest assured that in these three communities God is worshipped most devoutly, because they are inhabited by holy and exemplary monks. There is also a fine hospital to which poor people may be carried and where they are well cared for. It was founded by Miguel de Pasamonte, your Majesty's treasurer.

Day by day the city is growing larger and becoming more noble, and this is certain to continue since the Viceroy and your Majesty's high court of justice and Royal Chancellery are located there. Likewise, most of the rich people of the island live in or near the city of Santo Domingo.

## 3
## THE NATIVES OF HISPANIOLA

The natives of Hispaniola are somewhat smaller than Spaniards, and are of light brown color. Each Indian has his own wife and no man marries his daughter or his sister nor does he couple with his mother. They may couple with and marry women of any other degree of kinship. Those Indians have wide foreheads and very straight black hair. Neither the men nor women have beards or any hair on any part of their bodies. It is a very rare thing for either a man or a woman to have any hair on the body. They go naked as they were born, except that over their privates they wear a loincloth, of linen or some other kind of cloth, about the size of a man's hand. But this piece of cloth is not worn in such a way as to fulfill the purpose for which it is intended.

It seems advisable, before continuing further, to describe the bread and food of the Indians of that island, so that we shall have less to say about Tierra Firme, because the natives of both places have about the same foods.

## 4
## BREAD MADE FROM INDIAN CORN

In Hispaniola both Indians and Spaniards have two kinds of bread, for the Christians eat the same bread as the Indians. One sort is made of *maíz* [maize],[6] which is a grain, and the other of cassava, which is a root of the manioc. Corn is planted and harvested in the following manner. Corn is grain that is borne on an ear about six to eight inches long. This ear or spike is covered with grains almost as large as chickpeas. The Indians first cut down the cane and trees where they wish to plant it, for soil on which grass grows is not as fertile as

---

6. *Zea mays*. Henceforth 'maize' or 'Indian corn' will be called 'corn.'

the land covered with cane and trees. After the trees and cane have been felled and the field grubbed, the land is burned over and the ashes are left as a dressing for the soil, and this is much better than if the land were fertilized. An Indian takes in his hand a stick as tall as he is, and plunges the point into the earth, then he pulls it out, and in the hole he has made he places with his other hand about seven or eight grains of corn. Then he takes another step forward and repeats the process. He continues this procedure until he comes to the end of the field he is planting, continuing to plant grains of corn. On each side of the Indian are other Indians who form a line and do the same thing, and thus they go back and forth across the field until they finish the planting.

The corn sprouts within a few days and is harvested in four months; some of it may be harvested earlier, and often in as little time as three months. As the corn is sprouting, it is necessary to keep weeds and grass out of the fields until the corn is high and stands far above the grass and weeds. When the corn matures and the ears begin to fill out, it is necessary to protect it. Indian children, employed at this task, are placed in trees and on scaffolds built of canes and wood, with covers to keep off the rain and the sun. There they keep a sharp lookout for the many parrots that come to eat the grain, and they drive the birds away by shouting.

The cane or stalk on which corn grows is about as thick as a man's little finger, often smaller, sometimes larger. It usually grows taller than a man and the blades are like those of cane here in Spain, except that they are longer, more flexible, and not so rough and narrow. Each stalk bears one ear on which there are from two hundred to five hundred grains, more or less, according to the size of the ear. Some stalks bear two or three ears, and each ear is covered with three or four, never less than two, leaves or husks which fit close to the ear. These husks are somewhat rough and similar to the leaves of the stalk on which the ear grows. The ear is covered in such fashion that it is well protected from the elements. In this husk the ear ripens, and when it dries, the ear is plucked.

Parrots and monkeys do much damage to the corn crop if it is not protected. On the island the fields are safe from monkeys because, as I have already said, there is no quadruped except the *cori* and the *hutia*, and these two animals do not eat grain. Swine are very destructive on the islands and even more so in Tierra Firme, where there have always been wild pigs. There are also many deer and monkeys which destroy the cornfields. Therefore, because of birds as well as animals, it is necessary to keep vigilant and constant watch as long as the corn is in the field. This method of growing corn was learned from the Indians, and the Christians who live in the New World cultivate the grain in the same way.

One *fanega* of land[7] usually produces twenty to eighty, and in some areas more than one hundred, *fanegas* of corn.[8] When the grain has been harvested and stored in houses, it is eaten in the following fashion. On the islands the grain is roasted. Also when the ears are tender they are eaten almost like milk. The Christians feed it to their horses and stock, and it is fine feed for them. In Tierra Firme, however, the Indians prepare corn in a different fashion. The Indian women grind it, with full strength of their arms, in a concave stone with another round stone which they hold in their hands, just as painters are accustomed to grind their colors. As they grind, from time to time they pour in a little water which mixes with the meal. This produces a paste-like dough. A small portion of the dough is wrapped in a leaf which is used for this purpose, or in a corn husk, or in some other similar leaf. Then it is placed in the coals of a fire and baked. The dough becomes firm, takes on the color of white bread, and a crust forms on the outside. Inside, the crumb is somewhat softer than the crust. The bread must be eaten while it is hot, since it is not so palatable when it is cold, nor is it then easy to chew, for it becomes hard and bitter. These rolls are also boiled, but they are not so good as the baked bread. But boiled or baked, the bread remains fresh only a few days. After four or five days it molds and is not edible.

5

## BREAD MADE FROM YUCA

There is another kind of bread that is called *cazabi* [cassava], which is made from the root of a plant that the

---

7. 1.59 acres.
8. 1.58 bushels.

Indians call *yuca*.⁹ This is not grain, but a plant that sends up stalks taller than a man. The leaf is almost like that of hemp, like the palm of a man's open hand with the fingers extended. The leaves, however, are larger and thicker than those of hemp. To propagate this plant, the Indians break a branch of it into pieces about two spans long. Some men make small hills of earth at regular intervals and, as a border, just as it is done in this kingdom of Toledo, vine stocks are set around the hills. In each hill they place five or six or more of the cuttings of the plant. Other Indians do not go to the trouble to make hills but simply level the soil and insert these cuttings at regular intervals in the earth. Before planting the yuca, the natives grub or cut over the land and burn the brush, just as they do in preparing the land for planting corn, as described in the above chapter. After a few days the cutting buds for then it takes root.

As the yuca grows, the land is kept clean until the plant stands well above the weeds and grass. This plant is not damaged by birds, but it is often destroyed by swine. If it is the poisonous species, swine do not dare to eat it for it would kill them. But there is another species which is not poisonous and it is necessary to protect it from the rootings of hogs, because the fruit is produced on the roots of the plant. The fruit, which grows among the roots, is in the form of ears resembling large carrots, and often much larger than carrots, which have a rough rind and are tan in color. Inside, the fruit is white. In order to make bread of it, which is called cassava, the Indians grate it and then press it in a strainer, which is a sort of sack about ten palms or more in length and as big as a man's leg. The Indians make this bag from palms which are woven together as if they were rushes. By twisting the strainer as one does to remove the milk from crushed almonds, the juice is extracted from the yuca. This juice is a powerful and deadly poison, and one swallow of it will produce sudden death.

The residue after the liquid is removed, which is something like moist bran, is cooked in the fire in a very hot flat clay vessel of the size they want the loaf to be. The mash is spread out, taking care that none of the liquid remains

---

9. *Manihot utilissima.*

in it, then a loaf of the desired size is formed, which is necessarily the same size as the vessel in which it is baked. When the loaf has become firm it is removed from the fire and cured. Often it is placed in the sun. The Indians then eat it for it is very good bread. The liquid which is extracted from the yuca is boiled several times and left in the open for several days. Then it becomes sweet and is used as honey or other syrup to mix with other foods. Later this liquid is boiled and placed outdoors. It then turns sour and is used for vinegar without any danger whatsoever to the user.

This cassava bread can be kept for a year or more and can be carried from one place to another, even great distances, without spoiling or becoming stale. It is good food for sea voyages and it is carried by the Indians on all their trips, to the islands and to Tierra Firme, without becoming bad or soggy.

This species of poisonous yuca grows in great abundance on the islands of San Juan [Puerto Rico], Cuba, Jamaica, and Hispaniola. There is another species called *boniata*,[10] the juice of which is not poisonous. This species is eaten after it has been cooked like carrots, with or without wine, and it is very good food. In Tierra Firme all the yuca is the *boniata*, and I have eaten it many times, as I have said. In that land very few of the natives go to the trouble to make cassava of the roots. Ordinarily they eat it in the manner I have described, roasted in the hot embers of the fire, and in this way it is very good.

In some of the islands where the poisonous yuca[11] is found, occasionally there has been some Indian chief or leader and many of his subjects who have committed suicide. The chief, through the exhortations of the devil, would tell all those who wanted to die with him the reason that he thought would draw them to their diabolical end. Then each one would take swallows of the water or juice of the yuca and suddenly they would all die without any help whatsoever.

This yuca does not reach maturity nor is it harvested until it has grown in the fields for ten months or a year. When

---

10. Root of the yam.
11. The juice of cassava *(Manihot utilissima)* contains hydrocyanic acid, which is removed by boiling. For bibliography on cassava see L. W. J. Holleman and A. Aten, *Processing of Cassava and Cassava Products in Rural Industries*. Soil and climate determine whether cassava is 'bitter' or 'sweet.'

it has reached this age, the Indians harvest it and make use of it.

## 6
## OTHER FOODS OF THE INDIANS

Since we have already spoken of Indian bread, we should now speak of other foods of this island, except fruit and fish, with which the Indians sustain themselves. These will be discussed later on, since they are common to all the Indies. In addition to bread, the Indians eat *cories*[12] and *hutias*,[13] which have already been mentioned. The *hutias* are almost like rats, and certainly have some kinship with them. The *cories* are like rabbits or young conies. They are not vicious and are very pretty. Some are entirely white, while others are white spotted with red and other colors.

The natives also eat a kind of serpent that is very fierce and fearful to look upon but is entirely harmless. It is not certain whether this is an animal or a fish, since it lives in water, in trees, and on the ground. The quadruped[14] is larger than a rabbit and has a tail like a lizard's. The skin is spotted, although of different coloring. Its neck and spine are studded with erect spines. It has sharp teeth and tusks and a long, wide double chin which hangs down from its chin to its breast and which is of the same skin or hide. It is a quiet animal and does not howl, cry, or make any sound. It will remain tied to the foot of a chest, or anywhere else, without doing any harm or making any sound for ten, fifteen, or twenty days, and also without eating or drinking anything.

However, the Indians do feed it a little bread or something similar, which the animal will eat. The animal has four feet, long paws, well developed toes and claws as long as those of a bird, but weak and useless in capturing prey. This animal is better to eat than to see. There are very few men who have seen it alive who dare to eat it, except those in that land who are used to that fright and even greater ones. Really the animal is fearful only in appearance. The flesh is as good or better than rabbit. It is healthful except for those who have had syphilis. The meat is harmful to those who

12. *Cavia cobaya.*
13. *Capromys oedium.*
14. *Iguana tuberculata.*

have had that disease, even though they have been cured for a long time. I have heard this many times from many who have tried this food and who would have reason to know of what they spoke.

7

## BIRDS OF HISPANIOLA

I have not yet spoken of the birds of Hispaniola. On several occasions I have made the trip from the town of Yaguana to the City of Santo Domingo, a distance of more than eighty leagues, and nowhere have I seen fewer birds than on that island. Since all those I saw there are to be found on Tierra Firme, I shall describe them later in some detail. Here I shall say only that there are many Spanish hens and good capons. With regard to the native fruits and other plants and herbs, and the fish of the sea and of fresh water, I shall not attempt to place that here in the description of Hispaniola, because all of that is to be found more abundantly in Tierra Firme, and also many other things which will be discussed later.

8

## CONCERNING CUBA AND CERTAIN OTHER ISLANDS

All that I have said of the people and other things of Hispaniola applies in part to Cuba, Puerto Rico, and Jamaica. In all these islands the same things are to be found: gold and copper mines, cattle, trees and plants, fishes, and all other things which have been mentioned. There were no quadruped animals in any of those islands, just as in Hispaniola, until they were introduced by the Christians. At present there are many animals in all the islands and likewise much sugar cane and many drumstick trees[15] and all other things which have been mentioned.

On the island of Cuba there is a species of very small partridge[16] about the same as the turtle dove in plumage, but much more tasty. The natives capture many of these wild birds and bring them home alive, and within three or four days they are as tame as if they had been hatched in the

15. *Cassia fistula.*
16. *Columba cyanocephala.*

Indians' houses. They become quite fat and the meat is of a very delicate flavor. I think they are superior to our Spanish partridges since they are more easily digested.

But leaving aside all I have already said, there are two wonderful things in Cuba which have not been described or heard of previously. The first is a valley which extends for two or three leagues between two mountain ranges. The floor of the valley is covered with round balls of very hard stone. These stones are so perfectly round that by no mechanical means could they be made more smooth or round. They range from small ones, the size of a musketball, to very large ones. Some are large enough for any artillery, and if they should be desired of one-hundredweight, two-hundredweight, or larger, they could be found. These stones are to be found throughout the whole valley, as if it were a mine of them, and by digging they can be removed easily from the earth.

The other thing of wonder on the same island is that not far from the sea there flows from a mountain a liquid or bitumen-like pitch. It is sufficient in quantity and of good enough quality to tar ships. Since great quantities of this substance constantly flow into the sea, numerous rafts or patches of it float on the water from one place to another as moved by the wind or the currents along that coast where this bitumen or substance is to be found.

Quintus Curtius, in his fifth book, says that Alexander came to the city of Mennis, where there is a great cavern or cave in which there is a stream which flows with a great mass of pitch. Therefore it is easy to believe that the walls of Babylon could have been mortared with pitch, as the abovementioned writer has said.

This pitch is found not only on the island of Cuba but also in New Spain, recently discovered there in the province of Pánuco. This pitch is of finer quality than that to be found in Cuba, as experience has shown in the tarring of several ships.

But leaving this aside, I should continue with the main purpose I have in writing this report, which is to reduce to writing certain notable things concerning those regions, and to describe them for your Majesty, even though I may not remember every detail and may not be so thorough as I have been in another document I have written.

Before I turn to a description of Tierra Firme, however, I should like to describe a method of sea fishing employed by the Indians of Cuba and Jamaica, and also give a description of the manner in which they hunt or fish for wild geese. It is done in the following fashion: There are certain fish about a span long, or longer, that are called *pez reverso*[17] [remora]. They are ugly in appearance, but very courageous and clever. Often these fish are caught in nets with other fish, and I have eaten many of them. When the Indians wish to raise or keep these fish, they place them in sea water and feed them. When they want to fish with one, they take it to the sea in their *canoa* [dugout] or boat, and keep it there in a container filled with water. They tie a strong, thin cord to the fish and when they see a large fish, something like a turtle or a shad, for there are many in these waters, or any other fish that is swimming near enough to the surface to be seen, the Indian takes the remora in one hand and strokes it with the other, telling it in his native tongue to be brave and courageous and diligent, and speaking other words encouraging the fish to great effort. He tells the fish to be brave and to anchor itself to the largest and best fish it can find. At the right moment the Indian releases the fish and starts it towards the place where the large fish has been sighted. Then the remora darts straight as an arrow and fastens itself to one side or the belly of a turtle or some other large fish. When the large fish realizes that it has been seized by the small fish, it swims rapidly from one place to another.

Meanwhile the Indian lets out the full length of his long cord, to the end of which is tied a cork or a stick or some other light object which serves as a marker and remains on the surface. In a short time the fish or turtle to which the remora has fastened itself becomes tired and swims toward the shore. Then the Indian in his dugout or boat begins to wind in the cord, and when only a few feet or yards remain to be wound in, he begins to pull lightly and slowly, thus guiding the remora and the fish it has seized, until they are brought to the beach, about four to seven feet from dry land. The waves throw the fish out of the water, and the Indian seizes it and drags it to dry land.

17. Any of several fish of *Remora, Echeneis*, or related genera.

When the fish is out of the water, the Indian speaks many words of praise to the remora for what it has done, and carefully and slowly pulls it from the large fish. The remora is so tightly attached to the fish that if it were forcibly pulled away the remora would be torn to pieces. Some of the turtles which are caught in this fashion are so large that two Indians, and sometimes even six, have difficulty in carrying them on their backs to the town. Sometimes the remora catches some other larger fish. The remora is a real executioner or ferret for catching fish in the manner described.

The remora has scales arranged in the manner of steps, or in the same fashion as the hard palate or roof of the mouth of a man or a horse, and at that spot there are fine, hard, strong spines with which it fastens itself to the fish it wants to catch. It has these scales or small spines on most of the body surface.

With regard to the second point mentioned above, which is the taking of wild geese, your Majesty should know that at the time of migration these birds fly in great numbers over the islands. They are very beautiful, black with white breasts and bellies. Around their eyes are very red round warts, which appear to be real coral, and which are connected at the lachrymal caruncle as well as at the corner of the eye, on the side next to the neck, and from there they descend to the middle of the neck in a straight line, one attached to the other, several of these warts, six or seven or even a few more.

These geese light in large numbers on the lakes of the islands. The Indians who live there throw large round empty gourds[18] into the water. These float on the water and the wind drives them from one place to another and carries them even to the shore. At first the geese are frightened by the gourds and they rise and fly away. But when they see that the gourds are harmless, little by little they lose their fear. Gradually they become used to the gourds and pay so little attention to them that many of them become bold enough to light on the gourds and float about on the water moved by the air.

When an Indian knows that the geese are well used to and unafraid of the sight and motion of the gourds, he places one of them over his head and down to his shoulders, with the

---

18. Alvarez López identifies this goose as *Cairina moschata* and the gourd as *Crescentia cucurbitifera*, p. 200.

rest of his body under the water. Through a small hole he can see where the geese are, and he can approach them. From time to time one will light on the gourd. When the Indian knows this, he draws away slowly, swimming without being heard by the goose he carries or by any of the others. (Your Majesty must know that these Indians are the most expert swimmers.) When he is some distance from the other geese, and he thinks it is the right time, he puts out his hand and seizes the goose by the legs and pulls it under the water and holds it there until the bird is drowned. Then he ties it to his belt and returns to capture others in the same manner. In this way the Indians capture many geese. The other geese do not become frightened and fly away because they think these geese have dived beneath the surface to catch fish. The Indian, without leaving the spot, as soon as he knows that a goose has settled on the gourd, grabs it, as I have said, and pulls it under the water and ties it to his belt.

And may this suffice for things concerning the islands. With regard to their customs and riches, I shall not tarry here, but describe them in the general history I am writing in which nothing is to be written that has been known up to now.

Let us pass to what I recall and remember of Tierra Firme. But first, I happen to remember a plague that exists in Hispaniola and other islands inhabited by Christians, although it is not now so common as it was when those islands were first conquered. An insect smaller than the smallest flea penetrates the skin of the feet and forms a pocket as large as a chickpea between the skin and the flesh. It swells with nits, which are the eggs which the insect deposits. If it is not taken out in time the *niguas* (for that is the name of this small animal)[19] grow and increase so that the men are so seriously affected that they are crippled and remain lame forever. There is no remedy for this.

9

## TIERRA FIRME

The Indians of Tierra Firme are somewhat larger, stronger, and better formed than those of the islands. In some localities they are warlike and in others fairly peaceful. They fight with

---

19. Chigoe; *Sarcopsylla penetrans*.

various types of arms and in different manners, according to the custom of the place or province in which they live.

Their marriage customs are the same as those of the inhabitants of the islands, and in Tierra Firme the men do not marry their daughters, sisters, or mothers. Here I do not wish to speak of New Spain, although it is a part of Tierra Firme, because Hernando Cortés has described it in his *Letters* very fully as he saw it.[20]

I have also collected from eyewitnesses much material which is in my diary, since I have desired to inquire and to learn the truth, from the time Diego Velázquez first sent a captain from Cuba named Francisco Hernández de Córdoba, who discovered, or rather, first touched that land. (For the real discoverer was the first Admiral of the Indies, Christopher Columbus, father of Admiral Diego Columbus, through whose counsel and commands others have sailed through those places).

After the above-mentioned captain, Francisco Hernández, the governor sent Captain Juan de Grijalva, who explored more of that land and coast. Then Governor Diego Velázquez sent proof and specimens to your Majesty in Barcelona in 1519. The third man who went to that land at the request of the above-mentioned governor was Hernando Cortés. All this and more will be found in detail in my *General History of the Indies,* whenever your Majesty may be pleased to publish it.

So then, leaving New Spain, I shall describe some of the things which have been seen in the other provinces, or at least in those in the territory of Castilla del Oro and along the coast of the North Sea and something of the South Sea. There should be noted one singular and wonderful thing that I have observed of the Ocean Sea, concerning which no cosmographer, pilot, sailor, or native up to now has been able to satisfy me. It is this. As your Majesty well knows, and as everyone knows who has studied the sea and has considered its workings, that great Ocean Sea empties through the mouth of the Strait of Gibraltar, forming the Mediterranean Sea. The water in this sea from the Strait to the end of the Sea of the Levant neither rises nor falls on any coast or in any place. Therefore there are no tides, great flood tides, or ebb

---

20. Hernando Cortés described the conquest of Mexico in five letters (*Cartas de relación, 1519-26*) addressed to the Emperor Charles V. An accessible Spanish edition is *Cartas de relación de la conquista de Méjico*. An English version is *Five letters, 1519- 1526*, translated by J. Bayard Morriss.

tides, except in a very small way. From the Strait of Gibraltar over the whole Ocean Sea there is high tide and low tide every six hours, touching the entire coast of Spain, Brittany, Flanders, Germany, and England.

The same Ocean Sea on the northern coast of Tierra Firme neither rises nor falls for more than 3000 leagues, and the same is true with regard to Hispaniola, Cuba, and all the other islands that are to the north, except as it is found in Italy in the Mediterranean. This is insignificant when compared with the rise and fall of the tide on the coasts of Spain and Flanders.

Notwithstanding this, in the same Ocean Sea on the southern coast of Tierra Firme, in Panama and on the coast there opposite the east and west of the city and on the Island of Pearls, which the Indians call Terarequí, and on the Islands of Taboga and Otoque and all the others in the South Sea, the rise and fall of the tide is so great that at low tide the water almost disappears from view. I have seen this happen thousands of times.

Your Majesty should note one other thing. From the North Sea to the South Sea—and one is quite distinct from the other, as has been said regarding the rise and fall of the tides—there is a strip of land only eighteen or twenty leagues wide separating the two seas. So, since it is all the same sea, it is worth seeing and speculating on for those who have the inclination and desire to learn this secret. Since many learned persons have been unable to satisfy me or to explain the cause, I am satisfied that the one who can do so not only knows that but also many other things not given to the intelligence of average mortals, especially to such a small brain as mine. Let those who have better minds ponder what may be the real explanation.

In true terms and as an eyewitness, I have posed the question here and until it can be answered let us return to the main topic. I say that the river that the Christians call San Juan, in Tierra Firme, flows through seven mouths into the Gulf of Urabá, where it is called Culata [the delta]. And when the sea falls the little I have said on the northern coast, because of the said river, all the Gulf of Urabá, which is more than twelve leagues long and from six to eight leagues wide, turns fresh and the water can be drunk. I have tasted this water while I was anchored in a boat in seven fathoms of water and more than a league from the shore. So one can easily believe that this river is very large.

But neither this nor any river I have ever seen, heard of or read about, can compare with the Marañón [Amazon], which is in the east and on the same coast. Its mouth is forty leagues wide and for a great distance out to sea, fresh water can be dipped up from the river. I have heard this many times from the pilot Vicente Yáñez Pinzón, who was the first Christian to see the Marañón river. In a caravel he sailed more than twenty leagues up this river and discovered many islands and peoples. Since he had only a few men with him he did not dare to land. He then sailed from the said river, and forty leagues out to sea he dipped up fresh water. Other mariners have seen this river, but the pilot who learned most about it is the one I have mentioned.

That whole coast is covered with much brazil wood, and the natives are bowmen. The coast to the east and west of the Gulf of Urabá is high, and natives have different languages and weapons. The Indians of the coast to the west fight with sticks and wooden swords. The sticks or rods can be hurled and some are made of palm, others of heavier wood, and with sharp points. They are thrown with the full force of the arm. There are other weapons of reed grass or straight light canes, on the point of which they fix a flint tip or a point of heavier and harder wood. These weapons are thrown with leather thongs which the Indians call *estoricas*.

The *macana* is a heavy, two-edged staff somewhat less than four fingers wide, about as tall as a man. It is made of palm or other strong wood. The Indian wields these *macanas* as they would clubs, in both hands, and with them they can deliver heavy blows and inflict terrible wounds. They are so effective that they can stun any strong man even through his helmet.

In no regard are the Indians who use these weapons as warlike as those who use the bow and arrow. The bowmen inhabit the land from the Gulf of Urabá, or Caribana Point, to the east. Their coast is also high. These Indians eat human flesh; they are filthy, cruel, and they are also sodomites. They shoot arrows poisoned with an herb that is so poisonous that it is miraculous if a man wounded by such an arrow does not die. Usually the wounded man dies in delirium, chewing his own flesh and biting the earth.

From Caribana Point, the whole stretch of the coast of Cenú, Cartagena, the Coronados, Santa Marta, the Sierra Nevada, and as far as the Gulf of Cumaná and the Boca del Drago [Dragon's mouth], and all the islands that are near this coast, for a space of more than six hundred leagues, are inhabited by Indians that for the most part shoot poison-tipped arrows. Up to now no antidote for this poison has been discovered even though many Christians have died from it.

I suppose I should explain why I called them *coronados* [tonsured]. On a certain part of this coast all the Indians are shorn, with hair about as long as it would be three months after having the head shaved. In the middle of this short growth of hair there is a large, round tonsure like that on the head of an Augustinian monk. All these tonsured Indians are very strong and use the bow. They hold about thirty leagues of coast from Canoa Point to the large river, which they call Guadalquivir, near Santa Marta. Passing along this coast, more than six leagues at sea, I dipped up a cask of fresh water from this river.

I have been told by Indians that the poison that they use to tip their arrows is made from sweet-smelling apples [manchineel] and certain large ants, which will be described further on, and the venom of vipers, scorpions, and other poisonous ingredients which they mix. It appears to be very black pitch. In 1514 in Santa Marta, in a village about two leagues or more inland, I burned a great quantity of this poison, as well as many arrows and the house in which it was stored. This was at the time of the arrival of the fleet commanded by Pedrarias de Avila, which had been sent to Tierra Firme by Ferdinand the Catholic, God rest his soul.

I have already said that the food and manner of eating were practically the same on the islands and in Tierra Firme. That is true with regard to bread and most fruits and fishes. In Tierra Firme, however, there are more species of fruits and I believe there are more different kinds of fishes. There are also many strange animals and birds. But before I go into detail concerning those things I think it best to say something of the towns, dwellings, houses, ceremonies, and customs of the Indians. From this point on, then, I shall discuss the things that I remember about the people and the land.

## 10

### INDIANS OF TIERRA FIRME
### THEIR CUSTOMS, RITES, AND CEREMONIES

The Indians of Tierra Firme are of about the same size and color as those of the islands. Perhaps they are slightly larger, especially those I have described as being tonsured. Undoubtedly they are larger and stronger than any others I have seen in that section, except those who live on the Island of Giants [Curaçao], which is south of the island of Hispaniola near the coast of Tierra Firme.

There are others called Lucayos [Natives of the Bahamas] who live to the north of Hispaniola. Both these tribes of Indians, although not giants, are certainly the largest people discovered up to now. They are larger generally than the Germans, and many of them, women as well as men, are very tall. Both sexes use the bow, but they do not shoot poison-tipped arrows.

In some places of Tierra Firme the lord is called *quevi*, in other places *cacique, tiva,* and *guajiro,* and even other names, since there are many different languages among those peoples. But in a large province of Castilla del Oro, which is called Cueba, they speak a much better language than in other sections. Most of the land of Cueba has been conquered and there the Christians are in command and respected.

In this province one who is a principal personage, who has vassals but is inferior in rank to a *cacique,* is called *saco*. A *saco* has many Indian subjects, who own land and villages and who are called *cabra,* and they are something like gentlemen or grandees, separated from the common people, and are superior to others of the ordinary people whom they command.

The *cacique,* the *saco,* and the *cabra* have their own names, and likewise the provinces, rivers, valleys, and places where they live are named.

An Indian who is one of the common people may rise to be a *cabra* and attain this name or rank in the following fashion: when in some battle of a *cacique* or lord against another, an Indian fights bravely and is wounded, then the lord calls him *cabra* and gives him people to command, and he also gives him land or a wife or does him some signal favor for what he did in battle. From then on he is more honored than the others, and lives separate and apart from the common people, and his sons succeed him in rank and are called *cabras*, and they are required to follow the pursuits of war. The wife of such a man, in addition to her own name, is called *espave*, which means 'lady.' Likewise the wives of the *caciques* and other lords are called *espaves*.

These Indians build their villages near the sea or near the rivers or brooks where there are fish, which is ordinarily the chief item of food. They are very fond of fishing and catch fish in great abundance. This is better food than the wild pig and deer, which they also kill and eat.

The Indians fish with very good nets made of cotton. Nature has supplied them most abundantly with this plant and many forests and woods are filled with it. But when they want to improve the cotton and make it whiter, they plant and cultivate it in their fields or near the houses and villages in which they live.

They trap deer and pigs with branches and traps made of nets, into which the animals fall. At times they hunt and beat them out, and with a great number of people they attack them and take those that they can kill with arrows and spears. After they have killed the animals, since they do not have knives with which to skin them, they quarter them and cut them to pieces with stones and flints. They roast the flesh on sticks which they place in the ground, like a grating or trivet, over a pit. They call these *barbacoas*, and place fire beneath, and in this manner they roast fish also. Since this land is naturally hot, even though it is tempered by Divine Providence, fish and meat soon spoil if they are not roasted on the same day that they are killed or caught.

I have already said that the land is naturally hot, and tempered by God's Providence. It happens in this way: not without reason did the ancients consider the Torrid Zone, through which the equinoctial line passes, uninhabitable, since the sun is hotter there than on any part of the globe, because it lies between the Tropic of Cancer and the Tropic of Capricorn. It is obvious that the surface of the earth is temperate to a depth of several feet, and the trees and plants take root in that depth of soil and do not send their roots any deeper. Rather in that space they take root, and the roots spread out in the ground and become thicker than the branches above. They do not grow deeper than that layer of soil, for deeper the earth is very hot. The surface, however, is temperate and moist, as much from the great rains that fall from heaven during the rainy season and throughout the year as from the great number of large rivers, brooks, springs, and marshes with which God the King has supplied that land. There are also many tall mountains and mountain ranges, very cool breezes, and clear, comfortable nights.

The ancients, being ignorant of this, thought that the Torrid Zone and the equinoctial line were uninhabitable. All this I depose and affirm as an eyewitness, and I should be believed, and not those others who have a contrary opinion but have not seen that land.

The north coast of the gulf of Urabá and the port of Darién, where ships from Spain dock, is at six and one-half to eight degrees north latitude, except for several points stretching into the sea at the north, and there are few of these. The easternmost point of this new part of the world is Cape Santo Agostín.[21] This is at eight degrees south latitude.

Thus the distance from the equator to the gulf of Urabá is from one hundred twenty to one hundred thirty and three-quarter leagues, figuring seventeen and one-half leagues to one degree from poll to poll. Therefore this whole stretch of coast is about the same distance from the equator. Therefore in the city of Santa María del Antigua del Darién, and that whole gulf of Urabá, the days and nights are almost always equal. We are so close to the equator that the difference between day and night in twenty-four hours, or one day, is so slight that it is not noticed except by those who understand the sphere.

The North Star is very low, and when the stars in the handle of the dipper are straight down, they are below the horizon and cannot be seen. However, I should speak no further of irrelevant matters, but return to the main subject of this treatise.

21. The easternmost tip of Brazil.

I said above that it rains at regular times in that land, and it is true, and that summer and winter are just the reverse of those seasons in Spain. Here in Spain the worst of our winter in cold as well as rain is in December and January, and our summer or hottest season is around St. John's day and the month of July. It is just the reverse in Castilla del Oro. There the warmest and dryest season is a month before and after Christmas, and the wet season a month before and after St. John's day. The latter season is called winter, not because it is colder, nor warmer at Christmas, (for in that land the temperature is even throughout the year) but because it is the rainy season, and the sun is very rarely seen. Because of the many rains it seems to be cold when it really is not.

The *caciques* and lords among these Indians take as many wives as they desire, if they can find handsome ones who please them and who are women of rank, daughters of lords, and of their own nation and language. They do not care for foreign women. When they cannot find these, they take those who look best to them. The eldest son succeeds his father, and if there are no sons, the oldest daughter becomes the heir and is married to her leading vassal.

But if the oldest son is survived by daughters and not sons, the daughters do not become his heirs, but the sons of the second daughter, because they know definitely that she is of their family. Just as my sister's son most certainly is my nephew, and the son or daughter of my brother may be doubted to be his own.

The men take only one wife, and sometimes they may put her aside and take another, but this happens rarely. Very little ceremony is necessary for this, only the desire of the husband or both spouses is sufficient. This happens most often when the woman is barren. For the most part these women are virtuous, but there are some, especially high-born ladies, who give themselves to any man who wants them, saying that noble and high-born women should never refuse to grant anything requested of them. Only low-born women refuse.

On the other hand, the native women are careful not to mix with common people, unless they are Spaniards, whom they know to be very vigorous men and all of whom they consider noble. They recognize the difference and rank among Christians, especially in governors and others whom they see command other men. They are very fond of the Spaniards and consider themselves highly honored when they are loved by them. Many of these women, after they have known Christians carnally, will remain faithful to them unless they go too far away and remain too long, for they have no desire to be widows or nuns who protect their chastity.

When they become pregnant, many of the Indian women eat of an herb that moves and expels the pregnancy. They say the old women are the ones who should bear children. The young women do not want to give up their pleasures, or to become pregnant, because childbearing causes their breasts to become flabby. They have very beautiful breasts and are quite proud of them.

When an Indian woman bears a child, she goes to the river and bathes, and immediately the flow of blood and purgation ceases, and for a few days she does no work. The sexual organs of Indian women then contract so that the men who have had sexual intercourse with them say that they are so tight that it is with pain that a man may gratify his passion. Those who have not borne children seem to be almost virgins.

In some places they wear a cloth wrap that reaches from the waist to the knees, covering their sexual members. The rest of the body is entirely naked, just as they were born.

The chiefs wear a tube of gold, and the other men large snail's shells, in which they place the male organ. The rest of the body is naked, because the Indians do not feel that the human body is anything to inspire shame. In many provinces neither men nor women cover their sexual organs nor do they wear anything on any part of the body.

In the province of Cueba a woman is called *ira* and a man *chui*. This word *ira* for woman seems to be not so unsuited for many both in Spain and in the New World.[22]

The differences over which the Indians quarrel and go to battle are concerning who shall have the most land and power. They kill those they can and sometimes they take captives whom they brand and keep as slaves. Each master

---

22. *Ira* in Spanish means 'wrath.'

has his own brand and some masters pull out one front tooth of their slaves as a mark of ownership.

The bow-using Caribs, or the people of Cartagena, and most of those who live along that coast, eat human flesh. They do not take slaves, nor are they friendly to their enemies or foreigners. They eat all the men that they kill and use the women they capture, and the children that they bear—if any Carib should couple with them—are also eaten. The boys that they take from foreigners are castrated, fattened, and eaten.

In both war and peace they paint their bodies with *jagua*,[23] which is a tree which will be described further on, from which they make a black ink, and with *bija*[24] which is something red, from which they make balls as of red ochre. The *bija* is a finer color. They make themselves hideous and paint various figures on their faces and other parts of the body. This annatto dye is very difficult to remove until many days have passed. It tightens and contracts the flesh a great deal, and the Indians look good in it, and besides they like the appearance of the paint.

To begin their battles or fights, and for many other things that the Indians want to do, they have special men whom they respect highly and whom they call *tequina*. They call any man who excels in any art a *tequina*, whether he is the best hunter or fisherman or the best maker of nets, bows, or other things. For *tequina* means master. They also call *tequina* the one who is master of communications and intelligence with the devil. This *tequina* speaks with the devil and receives replies from him. He then tells the Indians what they must do, and he predicts the future. Since the devil is an old astrologer, he knows what the weather will be, and he knows the outcome of things and how nature rules them. And thus, by the result that naturally is to be expected he informs them of the future and gives them to understand that through his deity, or as lord of all and mover of everything that is and will be, he can foresee things of the future and what will come to pass, and that he causes the thunder, and makes the sun and rain, that he rules the weather, and that he gives or deprives them of food.

23. *Genipa americana.*
24. Annatto tree, *Bixa orellana.*

The Indians, deceived by the *tequina* since they have seen many of his prophecies come true, believe everything he says, and fear and respect him, and in certain places make sacrifices of blood and human lives, and in others of aromatic, fragrant, or foul-smelling smoke.

When God works contrary to the prediction, the *tequina* makes the Indians believe that he [the *tequina*] has changed the prophecy because of some vexation, or by some pretext or lie that appears suited, since he is well able to order and deceive the people, especially those poor ones defenseless against such a strong adversary.

The natives say that the *tuyra* really speaks to them. That is their name for the devil. In some places also they call Christians *tuyra*, believing that by that name they honor and praise them. In reality it is a proper name for some who have gone to the New World who, having cast aside their consciences and fear of either divine or human law, have done things characteristic not of Christians but of dragons and infidels. Maliciously they have caused the death of many Indians who could have been converted and saved. Even if those who died could not have been converted, they could have been useful to your Majesty and helpful to the Christians. And no part of the island would have been completely depopulated, for from the above cause it is almost uninhabited. Those who have perpetrated these crimes call the uninhabited places 'peaceful.' I feel they are more than peaceful; they are destroyed. But in this connection God is satisfied, and so is the world, with the sacred purpose and work of your Majesty. With the advice of many theologians, jurists, and men of high intelligence, you have provided and remedied with your justice everything possible with the reorganization of your Royal Council of the Indies, which now is made up of prelates, professional and learned men, priests, lawyers, all great in ability and men of conscience. I pray to Jesus Christ that all that up to now has gone wrong will be mended with their prudence and that the future will be such that our Lord will be served, and your Majesty likewise, and your Spanish kingdoms enriched and increased through respect for those lands, since God has made them so rich and preserved them for you from the time of creation, in order to make of your Majesty the universal and only monarch in the world.

Returning to the subject of the Indian *tequina*, who speaks to the devil and through whose hand and advice all those diabolical sacrifices, ceremonies, and rites are performed, I say that neither the ancient Romans, nor the Greeks, nor the Trojans, nor Alexander, nor Darius, nor other princes of old, since they were not Catholics, were free from these errors and superstitions. Since they were so governed by those soothsayers and augurers, and so subject to the errors, vanities, and surmises of their mad sacrifices, in which the devil at times intervened, they conjectured right and forecast a part of what the future held, without knowing anything surely except what that common adversary of human nature taught them, in order to bring and drag them to perdition and death. And consequently when the sacrifice failed, they made excuses or gave cautious and equivocal answers, saying that the gods whom they worshipped were angry.

Since your Majesty has been in the city of Toledo, the pilot Estéban Gómez arrived there in the month of November last year, 1524, at your Majesty's command. He sailed toward the north and found there a great expanse of land that is called *Bacallao* [Cape Cod area], extending towards the west and located at about forty to forty-one degrees north latitude. From there he brought some Indians who are still in the city. On the average, I think these Indians are larger than those in Tierra Firme, and the pilot says that he has seen many as large as these. They are of the same color as those of Tierra Firme. They are expert bowmen, and dress in the skins of deer and other animals.

In that land there are excellent sable[25] and other rich fur-bearing animals. The above mentioned pilot brought some of these skins back with him.

According to what these Indians say and what we can gather from the signs they make, they have silver and copper, and worship the sun and the moon. Therefore they probably practice other idolatries, as do the Indians in Tierra Firme.

But to return to a consideration of the customs and errors of the Indians, it should be noted that in many places of Tierra Firme when a *cacique* or some lord dies, all the retainers of his household, both men and women, kill themselves. The devil

---

25 *Mustela zibellina*.

has led them to believe that those who commit suicide when the chief dies will go with him to heaven and there serve him food and drink or continue the same work they have done in the home of the *cacique* on earth.

Those who do not do this, they believe, when they die of some other cause, or naturally, their spirits die with the body. And all the other Indians and vassals of the chief, when they die, as has been said, their spirits die with the body. And so they die and are converted into air or into nothingness, as would happen to a pig, a bird, a fish, or any other animal. They believe that only the servants and vassals who serve the master in the house or in some particular service have and enjoy that right and pre-eminence.

From that false belief it results that even those who are engaged in the cultivation of corn kill themselves in order to enjoy this blessing, and have themselves buried with a little corn and a small wooden sword. The Indians say that it is carried with them so that if in heaven there is a lack of seed, they will have enough to begin their trade, until the devil, who informs them of everything, provides them with a larger quantity of seed.

In the highlands of Guaturo I was able to observe this very well. There I held prisoner the *cacique* of that province who had rebelled against the service of your Majesty. I asked him to explain to me the meaning of a number of graves that were in his house. He said that they were the graves of Indians who had killed themselves when his father died. Since often they are buried with great quantities of wrought gold, I had two of the graves opened. There I found the corn and knives that I mentioned above. When I asked the reason, the *cacique* and some of his Indians said that those who had been buried there were farmers, men who knew well how to plant and harvest corn, and they were his and his father's servants. And so that their souls would not die with their bodies, they had killed themselves upon the death of his father, and had the corn and knives for use in heaven.

I replied that the *cacique* should observe that the devil had deceived him, and that everything he told them was false, for those servants had been dead a long time and still had not carried away the corn and the knives. I also pointed out that now the seed was rotten and worthless, and that the dead had not planted anything in heaven. To this the *cacique* replied that if they had not carried those things away, it was because they had found plenty in heaven and those were not needed. They were told many things about this error of theirs, from which they profit little, to remove them from their way of error, especially when they are grown men and the devil already has them ensnared.

The Indians depict the ways the devil appears, when he talks to them, in a variety of forms and colors. They also make those figures of gold relief and carved on wood, very frightful and always ugly, and in as many different ways as our artists may paint him at the feet of Saint Michael the Archangel, Saint Bartholomew, or any other place they may paint the terrifying figure.

When the devil wishes to frighten the Indians he predicts a *huracán* [hurricane], which means storm. These storms are so fierce that they tear down houses and uproot many large trees. I have seen thick forests of very large trees torn down for the space of half a league, and a quarter of a league wide. Both large and small trees had been blown down, and the roots of many of the trees were above the ground. It was a terrible thing to see and could not be looked upon without great fear. Without doubt this destruction appeared to the Indians the work of the devil.

In this regard every Christian should contemplate the fact that everywhere Holy Communion has been celebrated, these hurricanes and terrific storms have not occurred in large numbers, nor are they as destructive as they used to be.

In some parts of Tierra Firme, when a *cacique* dies it is the custom to place his body on a stone or a log, and around him and very near, without coal or flame touching the body of the dead man, a large fire is built and kept going until all the grease and fluid comes out through the fingernails and toenails, and in sweat, and the body becomes so dry that the skin fits tight to the bones, and all the tissue and flesh are consumed. When the body is thus dried out without opening it (which is unnecessary) it is placed in a secluded spot in the house prepared especially for it, next to the body of the father of the *cacique*, which has been placed there in the same fashion.

And so, by seeing the number of the dead, one knows how many masters there have been in that province, and which was the son of another, since they are placed in order in the burial niches.

Of course it is obvious that if any of these *caciques* died in battle on land or on sea, in some place where his men could not carry his body home to be buried with the other *caciques,* then the correct number would not be known. In such case, in order to supply the memory and their lack of a written language, the sons of the *cacique* are required to memorize the manner of death of those who died in such a way that they could not be buried there. Then they sing of these matters in their songs which are called *areitos* [Indian songs].

Since I have said they have no alphabet, before I forget it I should say just how frightened they are at ours. I mean that when some Christian sends a message by an Indian to some other person who is in another place or far from the place where the message was written, the Indians are astonished to see that at the other place the letter means what the Christian who sends it wants it to mean. Consequently the Indians carry messages with much respect and care for they believe that the letters will be able to tell what the messengers did along the way. And often the stupidest of these Indians believe that these letters are living things.

The *areito* is something that may be described as follows: when the Indians want to amuse themselves and sing, a great company of men and women get together and catch hands, alternately men and women. The leader, who is called *tequina,* man or woman, takes a few steps forward and then back, something like a contradance, and they go around in this fashion, and he sings in a low or medium voice anything that he cares to, making the measure of his voice keep time with the steps. And what he speaks is repeated by the multitude that takes part in the contradance or *areito,* and the same steps and order, but in a louder voice. This goes on for three or four hours or longer, or from one day to another. At the same time there are other people who walk behind those who are dancing, giving them wine which they call *chicha,* which will be described further on. They drink so much that often they get so drunk that they appear to lose all senses. In these drunken orgies they tell how the *caciques* died, as was mentioned above, and they also sing of other things that may strike their fancy. And often they order their treason against those they love.

Sometimes the *tequinas* or leaders who direct the dance are changed, and the new guide of the dance changes the tune and the contradance and the words.

This type of song-dance is very similar to the form of the songs used among the farmers and villagers when in summer men and women for the pleasure join in the *panadero* [a clog dance]. In Flanders I have seen this form of song-dance also.

I shall now describe the *chicha*, or wine, which the Indians drink, and their manner of making it. They take a quantity of corn, according to the amount of *chicha* they desire to make, and put it to soak. There it remains until it swells and begins to sprout. Then there appear some small shoots on the part where the grain was attached to the ear on which it grew. As soon as the grain has sprouted, it is boiled in water, and when it has been boiled several times, the kettle or pot in which it is cooked is removed from the fire and the liquid is left to settle. It cannot be drunk on the first day. On the second day it begins to settle and can be drunk. On the third day it is good, because it all has settled, but on the fourth day it is best. On the fifth day it begins to sour, on the sixth day it is even more sour, and on the seventh it is not good to drink. Therefore they always make the quantity that will suffice up to the time it spoils. During the time that this drink is at its best it is much better than apple wine or cider, and it is also my opinion and that of others that it is better than beer. It is very healthful and mild. The Indians consider this beverage one of their chief staples, and it keeps them quite healthy and fat.

The houses in which the Indians live are of several styles. Some are round like pavilions and are called *caney*. In Hispaniola there is another type of house, built over the water. In Tierra Firme these are called *bohios*. Both are made of substantial framing, with walls of canes tied with lianas, which are round vines or filaments that grow on large trees and interlaced with them. The lianas are all sizes and sometimes the natives cut and prepare those they need to tie the timber and supports of the house. The walls are made of canes placed close together, plastered over with earth four or five fingers thick, and extend to the top of the house. This makes a substantial and handsome wall. The houses are covered with straw or long grass, which is well placed and lasts a long time. Rain does not enter these houses, for the roof affords as good protection as tile.

The lianas that are used as thongs are very well pounded, and the juice is extracted and strained, which the Indians use as a purge. I have also seen some Christians take this purge, and it is very agreeable for it cures them and is neither dangerous nor violent. Their way of covering houses is the same as that used in the hamlets and villages of Flanders. If one is superior or better installed than the other, I believe it is that of the Indies, since the straw or grass is much better than that of Flanders.

The Christians are now building houses with garrets and windows, since they have a stock of nails, using good boards which they saw themselves. These houses are so good that any gentleman could live comfortably for a long time in any one of them. In the city of Santa María del Antigua of Darién, I built a house that cost me more than 1,500 *castellanos*, and it is so comfortable that I could receive a great noble and put him up quite comfortably. I could live very happily in it because it has many high spacious rooms upstairs and downstairs. There is also a garden with many sweet orange trees, bitter orange trees, citron and lemon trees, for there are many of these trees where the Christians have settled. In the garden there is a beautiful stream, and the spot is attractive, healthful, and cool and enjoys a beautiful view along the banks. But to the misfortune of us who live there, as a result of the malicious plotting of one man, the town has been abandoned. But I shall not speak of it here since your Majesty has provided and ordered your Royal Council of the Indies to do justice so that those who have been offended may receive satisfaction. Time will tell what the outcome will be, and may God direct the matter according to your Majesty's saintly desire.

The third type of house is found in the province of Abrayme, which is in Castilla del Oro. There many Indian villages are built in trees, for on the tops they build their houses and dwellings. Each Indian has his own rooms, in which he lives with his wife and children. Steps are tied to the trees with lianas or cords made of lianas, and a woman can climb one of these trees with her child in her arms as easily as she could walk on level ground. The earth under the tree-houses is marshy and covered with shallow water less than six feet deep.

In some places these lakes are deep and there the Indians use dugouts, which are boats made of hollowed logs and of any size that they desire. They go from their dwellings to the dry land that has been cleared to plant their corn fields, yuca, sweet potatoes, chili peppers, and the other things they use for food. Those Indians live in such villages in order to be secure from animals, wild beasts, and their enemies, and to be safer, and without any danger from fire.

These Indians do not use bows but they fight with sticks, which they have in great quantities and which for their safety and defense they keep in their houses. So that from there they may defend themselves or attack their enemies.

They have another type of house especially on the large river of San Juan (which above I said flowed into the gulf of Urabá), in the middle of which there are many palm trees growing close together, and on the top of them they build fortified houses, like those in Abrayme described above except a great deal larger. There many people live together, and keep their dugouts tied at the foot of the palm trees so that they can go ashore and return as they please. These palm trees are so hard and strong and difficult to cut that it would be with great labor that one could damage them. The people who live in these river houses also fight with sticks. And the Christians who came there with the Governor Vasco Núñez de Balboa and other captains received much damage but they could inflict none upon the Indians, and they returned with the loss and death of a large number of their men. May this suffice for a description of their houses.

The houses in the villages are different because some villages in one area are larger than those in other places, and ordinarily the people live scattered over the valleys, on the slopes and in other places, and on top of the mountains. Sometimes they live near the rivers and sometimes away from them, and scattered around as they are in Biscay and in the mountain district, the houses being far apart. Many houses and much land belong to a *cacique* who is obeyed, served, and respected by his people. When he eats in the field or in the village, all the food is placed in front of him and he distributes it to the people, and gives to each one what he cares to. He also has certain men who farm for him, others who hunt and fish.

Sometimes the *cacique* takes part in these activities or in some pursuit that pleases him, unless he is at war.

The beds in which they sleep are called *hamacas* [hammocks], which are pieces of well-woven cotton cloth and of good and pretty tapestry. Some of them are very thin. They are two or three yards long, and somewhat narrower. On the end they are covered with long cords made of *cabuya* [century plant] and of *henequén* [sisal hemp]. These cords or filaments

*Una Hamaca—A Hammock*

will be described later. These cords are long and are joined together at the ends and in a stop knot as on the slot at each end of a crossbow. They tie each end to a tree, with cotton cords or rope which they call *hicos*. This bed hangs four or five palms from the ground like a sling or a swing. These beds are very clean and one can sleep quite comfortably in them.

Since the climate is temperate it is not necessary to use any cover. It is true that when sleeping in some mountain regions where it is cold, or upon coming home wet or damp, they usually put a fire beneath the hammocks to warm themselves. The cords with which they tie the ends of the hammocks are twisted ropes and well made of very good cotton, and of the most suitable size. When they do not sleep in the open, tying the hammocks between two trees, they tie them in their houses between two posts, for there is always a place to hang them.

All those Indians, men as well as women, are good swimmers, for from the time they are born they practically live in the water. To understand how skillful those Indians are in swimming it is necessary only to refer to what I have already said concerning the way the Indians of Cuba and Jamaica capture wild geese.

I said above that I would describe the threads of the century plant and of henequen. From the leaves of a certain plant, which is like lilies or cattail, they make these threads of the century plant or of henequen, which is the same thing except that henequen is very thin and is made of the best part of the plant and is something like flax, and the other is coarser. Between the two there is the difference between fine hemp and rough hemp. The color is somewhat golden and in some cases almost white.

With the henequen, which is the smallest of this thread, the Indians, if they so desire, can cut fetters or a bar of iron in this manner. As one cuts or uses a saw they move the henequen back and forth over the piece of iron that is to be cut, pulling the thread first one way and then the other, and sprinkling very small particles of sand on the spot where the thread touches the iron, thus wearing away the iron by friction. And when one thread wears out it is replaced by a strong new thread and the cutting is continued. In this way the Indians can cut a piece of iron, however thick it may be, and they cut it as if it were soft or something easily cut.

I also happened to think of something that I have observed many times with regard to these Indians. Their skulls are four times thicker than those of the Christians. And so when one wages war with them and comes to hand to hand fighting, one must be very careful not to hit them on the head with the sword, because I have seen many swords broken in this fashion. In addition to being thick, their skulls are very strong.

I have noticed that when the Indians realize they have too much blood they cut themselves on the calf of the leg and on their arms, between the elbows and hands, on the widest part above the wrist. Very sharp flints are used for this purpose. Sometimes the very sharp fangs of snakes or small reeds are used to make the incision.

Ordinarily these Indians are without beards, and it is very rare that either the men have beards or that men or women have any hair or down on any part of their bodies. However, the *cacique* of the province of Catarapa, whom I have seen, had a beard and also hair on other parts of his body where it is wont to grow, and also his wife had hair where woman usually have it. They say that in that province there are some, but very few, who have this, according to what the chief himself told me. He said that he had inherited it from his ancestors.

This chief painted a large part of his body with black permanent designs, as the moors in Barbary, especially the women, wear for ornament on their faces, throats, and other parts of the body. Among the Indians, the principal men have these designs on their arms and chests. Only slaves have them on their faces.

When the Indians of some provinces, especially the arrow-shooting Caribs, go into battle, they carry large snail shells which they blow in the fashion of hunting horns, and also drums, and many beautiful feather decorations, and some armor of gold, especially large round pieces on their chests, and bracelets, and other pieces on their heads and other parts of their bodies. Never are they so proud to be gentlemen and to be decked out in finery of gold and feathers as when they go to war.

From these snail shells they make small white beads of different shapes, and others red, black, and purple, and small tubes of the same material. They also make bracelets, mixed with alternate beads of shell and gold, which are worn on the wrists and above the ankle and below the knees for decoration. The principal women, who are proud of their beauty, wear all these things in the places I have said and also around their necks. They call these strings of beads and other trinkets *chaquira*. Besides all this they wear gold rings in their ears and in their noses, with a hole made from one nostril to the other, and the ring hanging down over the lips.

Some Indians crop their hair, although most of the men and women are proud of their hair and wear it long, hanging down below their shoulders. They trim the ends evenly and cut it in a straight line above the eyebrows. They are able to cut it very easily and evenly with flints.

When the principal women see that their breasts are sagging, they support them with a rod of elaborately wrought gold about a palm and a half long. Some of these rods weigh more than two hundred *castellanos*. A small hole is drilled through each end, through which are fastened cotton cords. One end of the cord goes over the shoulder and the other under the arm pit, where the two ends are tied. Some of the principal women go into battle with their husbands. When they are mistresses of the land, they command and lead their own men, as I shall explain further on.

Always the principal *cacique* has a dozen of the strongest Indians whose duty it is to carry him along the journey. He reclines in a hammock tied to a long light pole, and the Indians go running or half trotting with the pole on their shoulders. When the two who carry him get tired two others take their places and without stopping they continue the journey. In one day, if the land is level, they can cover in this way fifteen or twenty leagues. The Indians who have this duty are for the most part slaves or *naborías*. A *naboría* is an Indian who is not a slave, but he is forced to serve whether he wants to or not.

It may appear that I have not explained these things in sufficient detail, but since these and many others are fully and copiously described in my *General History of the Indies*, I want to pass on to other things that I mentioned in the introduction. First I shall speak of certain land animals, and especially of those that I remember most clearly.

## 11

### CONCERNING ANIMALS, AND FIRST THE TIGER

The tiger, according to the writers of antiquity, is the swiftest of all land animals. *Tiguer* in Greek means 'arrow.' Because of its swiftness the Tigris River was given that name. The first Spaniards who saw these tigers [jaguar, *Felis onca*] in Tierra Firme gave them that name, and they are like the one in the city of Toledo, which Admiral Diego Columbus gave your Majesty and which was brought to him from New Spain. The head is shaped like that of a lion or a lynx, but large. The whole body and legs are covered with black spots, close together, outlined in red, which makes for a beautiful marking. On the back and sides these spots are larger, being smaller on the belly, legs and head. The one that was brought here was small and young, about three years old, I believe.

In Tierra Firme there are much larger ones, for I have seen some more than three palms tall,[26] and more than five long. They have very strong legs, teeth, fangs, and claws.

---

26. Two feet. A palm is eight inches.

They are so fierce that I do not believe any of the biggest royal lions is as strong or as fierce.

There are many of these animals in Tierra Firme, and they eat many Indians and do other damage. But I cannot determine whether they are tigers, in view of what is written about the swiftness of the tiger and what I have seen of the slowness of the animals we call 'tiger' in the Indies.

It is true from what one can see of the marvels of the world and the great differences among animals, that these differences are greater in some places than in others, according to the locality or the constellations under which these animals have been bred. We see that the plants which are poisonous in some areas are healthful and useful in others; and that birds in one province are of good flavor while in other places they are not prized or eaten. Some men are black, while in other lands they are very white. Still they are all men. Granted all this, it may also be true that tigers in one place may be swift, and that in your Majesty's Indies under discussion here they may be slow and awkward. Likewise the men of some kingdoms are courageous and bold while in others they are cowardly and timid.

All these things, and many others that could be said in this connection, can easily be proved, and should be believed when they have been related by men who have read widely or who have traveled about the world. Their own experience has proved what has been said.

The yuca of the island of Hispaniola is a famous plant. The Indians make bread of it; they kill with its juice; and they dare not eat of its fruit. But in Tierra Firme it does not have such properties. I have eaten it several times and it has good fruit.

The bats in Spain, although they bite, do not kill nor are they poisonous. But in Tierra Firme many men have died from their bites, as will be described farther on. So we could speak of many things, but no one would have time to read them.

My purpose is to say that this animal may be a tiger, but not as swift as the tigers described by Pliny and other writers. These animals on Tierra Firme are easily killed by crossbowmen in the following fashion: As soon as the hunter learns where a tiger is, he stalks the animal with his crossbow and a small dog that hunts by scent or a hound. He does not hunt with a dog of prey because the tiger would easily kill any dog that attacks him, since he is a strong and powerful animal. As soon as the small dog comes upon the tiger he runs around barking, snapping at the animal, then retreating. In this way the animal is so harassed that he climbs the nearest tree. The tiger, molested by the dog, climbs to the top and remains there, while the dog at the foot of the tree continues to bark as the tiger shows his fangs.

When the hunter arrives he shoots an arrow from a distance of twelve or fifteen paces. The arrow strikes the animal in the breast, and the hunter runs away. The wounded tiger, left in his agony, bites the earth and trees. After two or three hours, or possibly the next day, the hunter returns with his dog to locate the dead animal.

In the year 1522 I and other councilmen of the city of Santa María del Antigua of Darién passed in our City Council an ordinance in which we promised to pay four or five gold pesos to anyone who would kill one of these tigers. As a result of this bounty, within a short time many tigers were killed in the manner described above and others were caught in traps.

In my opinion these animals are not tigers, nor are they panthers or any other of the numerous known animals that have spotted skins, nor some new animal that has a spotted skin and has not been described. The many animals that exist in the Indies that I describe here, or at least most of them, could not have been learned about from the ancients, since they exist in a land which had not been discovered until our own time. There is no mention made of these lands in Ptolemy's *Cosmography,* nor in any other work, nor were they known until Christopher Columbus showed them to us—a deed certainly greater and more hazardous than that of Hercules in creating an inlet to the Mediterranean from the Atlantic, a sea unknown to the Greeks before this feat. From this arose the fable concerning the mountains Calpe and Abila (which stand at the Strait of Gibraltar, one in Spain, the other in Africa, opposite each other) which says that they were one, and Hercules parted them, allowing the Atlantic to enter, and that he placed his two columns in Cadiz and in Sevilla, which your Majesty uses as your emblem, with your motto *Plus ultra.* These are words indeed worthy of our great and universal Emperor and not appropriate to any other prince, for your Catholic Majesty has placed them in strange lands thousands of leagues farther than Hercules or any other prince has ever come. Since Hercules navigated that ocean only a small distance, and therefore poets say he made the door to the ocean, etc., certainly, Sir, even if a gold statue should be made in honor of Christopher Columbus the Ancients would not have thought that sufficient, had he lived in their time.

But returning to the subject already begun, I say that the shape and appearance of this animal—and your Majesty has seen it, for there is now a live one in this city of Toledo—is just as I have already described it. But the lionkeeper of your Majesty has the idea of taming the animal, and I am sure he could employ his time more profitably and usefully. This tiger is young, and each day he will become more strong and fierce and his cunning will double. This animal is called by the Indians *ochi*, especially in Tierra Firme, in the province which our Catholic Sovereign Ferdinand ordered to be named Castilla del Oro.

Many days since I wrote the above, the above-mentioned tiger tried to kill the one who was in charge of him. The keeper had taken the animal, now apparently tame, from the cage and had tied him by a slender rope and was so familiar with him that I was dumbfounded to see it, for I knew that such gentleness would be of short duration and that some day the animal would kill his keeper. Shortly afterwards the tiger died, or perhaps was killed. In truth, those animals should never live among people, since they are fierce and by their very nature indomitable.

12

BEORI

The Christians in Tierra Firme gave the name *danta* [tapir][27] to an animal that the Indians call *beori* [American tapir]. It is because the coats of these animals are very thick, but they are not tapirs. Thus inappropriately they have named the *beori* 'tapir,' just as they have called the *ochi* 'tiger.'

The *beori* is about as large as a medium-sized mule; it has

---

27. American tapir, *Tapirus terrestris*. There are two American genera: *Tapirus terrestris* (Brazil) and *Tapirella bairdi* and *T. dowi* (Central America).

a brown coat that is thicker than the coat of the wild ox. It has no horns, although some people call them cows. The flesh is very good, but somewhat softer than Spanish beef. The feet of this animal are very good eating and quite tasty. It is necessary, however, to cook them twenty-four hours. After that time, it is a dish for an epicure.

They kill these tapirs with dogs. After the dogs have seized one of the animals, the hunter must save it by spearing it very quickly before it enters the water, if any is nearby. Once in the water, it turns on the dogs and kills them with great bites, often biting off a whole leg and half the shoulder of a whippet or tearing off a large part of his hide as if the dog had been skinned. I have seen both. However, they are not so well able to protect themselves on land. We have not yet learned how to tan the hides of these animals, and consequently the Christians do not make use of them. But the hide is as thick or thicker than that of the wild ox.

## 13

## OCELOT

The ocelot[28] is a very fierce animal, and has about the same shape and color as the small gray tame cats we have in Spain. But it is as large or larger than the tiger spoken of above. It is the fiercest animal in that land and the one the Christians fear most, and it is swifter than all other animals that have been discovered there.

## 14

## LION

In Tierra Firme there are royal lions [cougars][29] exactly like those in Africa. But they are somewhat smaller and not so bold. Rather, they are timid and flee. But that characteristic is common to lions, for they are not dangerous unless pursued or attacked.

## 15

## LEOPARD

There are also leopards[30] in Tierra Firme, similar in shape and appearance to those to be seen here and those of Africa.

28. *Felis pardalis.*
29. *Felis concolor.*
30. This is really the jaguar, *Felis onca.*

They are fierce and swift. But neither these nor the lions have harmed the Christians up to now. Nor do they eat the Indians, as do the tigers.

### 16
### FOXES

There are foxes[31] of the same appearance as those of Spain, but not the same color. Those in the Indies are darker than black velvet. They are very swift, but smaller than those in Spain.

### 17
### DEER

There are many deer[32] exactly like those in Spain, in color, size, and other features. But they are not so swift, to which I can bear witness, for several times I have chased and killed them with dogs. I have also killed them with the crossbow.

### 18
### FALLOW DEER

There are likewise very many fallow deer,[33] especially in the province of Santa Marta. They are of the same shape and size as those in Spain. In flavor, the fallow deer as well as the deer are as good or better than those in Spain.

### 19
### SWINE

Many of the swine carried from Spain to the New World have become wild on the islands and also in Santo Domingo, Cuba, San Juan [Puerto Rico] and Jamaica. The swine carried to Tierra Firme that have escaped to the forests have not lived long, for they have been eaten by the tigers, ocelots, and cougars. There are, however, many wild swine native to Tierra Firme, and they are often seen in large herds.[34] Since they travel in herds, other animals do

---

31. *Vulpes virginianus* or *Urocyon virginianus* or *U. cinereoargentatus*.
32. This is probably *Odocoileus virginianus* or *Cariacus virginianus*.
33. *Cariacus rufinus*
34. The peccary. *Dicotyles tajacu* and *Dicotyles labiatus*, or *Pecari angulatus* and *Tayassus pecari*.

not dare attack them. These pigs, however, do not have tusks like those from Spain, but they kill our dogs by biting them savagely. The swine are somewhat smaller than ours, and are covered with thicker hair or wool. They have the navel in the middle of the spine, and the back hoof is not cloven. Otherwise, they are like the swine in our own land.

The Indians call a pig *chuche* and catch them in traps and kill them with spears. When the Christians come upon a herd of pigs they try to get up on a rock or the trunk of a tree, even if it be no more than three or four palms high, and from there they wound two or three, or as many more as they can, with lance thrusts as they pass. And sparing the dogs, they capture a few in this way. But these animals are very dangerous when encountered in herds, if there is no elevated place from which the hunter may attack them, as I have said. Sometimes they are found when the females have gone aside to bear their young. Then the suckling pigs are captured. There are many of these and they have a very fine flavor.

20

## ANTEATER

In coat the anteater[35] is very much like our bear, except that it does not have a tail. It is smaller than the bears in Spain, and about the same in appearance except that it has a very much longer snout, and can see very poorly.

They are very easily captured by beating, and they are not dangerous. They are very easily taken with dogs, but it is necessary to be very quick to rescue the animals before the dogs kill them, for they are not able to defend themselves even though they can bite a little.

Most often they are found near large anthills that are made by a certain species of small black ants in the level countryside and fertile plains where there are no trees. Through fear of this animal the ants go there to breed by natural instinct, away from the forests. The anteater, since he is cowardly and defenseless, lives in wooded places and thickets until hunger and need, or the desire to feed upon ants, force him to go to the open spaces to look for them.

---

35. *Myrmecophaga jubata* or *Myrmecophaga tetradactyla* or *Cycloturus didactylus*.

These ants make an anthill about as tall as a man, sometimes taller, sometimes smaller, and about as thick as a large chest, sometimes the size of a large barrel, and as hard as stone. These anthills resemble mounds used as landmarks and boundary marks in Spain. Under the very hard earth with which these hills are made are very many exceedingly small ants, which can be caught by the gallon when the hill is broken open. After a rain, when the ground is soaked, and afterwards in the heat of the sun, the anthills often crack and very small fissures are formed. These cracks are as thin as a knife blade, and could not be thinner.

It seems that nature has given these ants the intelligence to be able to select the right clay with which to build their very hard anthills, for they really are as hard as mortar. I have tested them and have had them broken open. It is difficult to realize how hard they are without seeing them, because with pickax and iron bars it is very difficult to break them open. In order to learn more about this secret, I have had anthills broken open in my presence.

The ants build these hills for protection against their enemy the anteater, because this animal feeds principally upon ants, or the animal is given to these ants as a rival or enemy so that the proverb 'There is no creature so free that does not have its own enemy' shall be fulfilled. This enemy that nature gave to such small animals employs these means to get the hidden ants and kill them. The anteater goes to an anthill and places his tongue on one of the small cracks as thin as the edge of a sword, and by licking he moistens the crack, however small it may be. Its saliva is of such nature and the animal's persistence in licking so great, that little by little the fissure is enlarged, so that very easily and leisurely the anteater can insert and withdraw his tongue, which is very slender and very long in comparison with the size of his body. After the opening is to his liking, he places his tongue as far as he can in the hole he has made, and leaves it there quite a while. Since ants are very fond of moisture a great many get upon the anteater's tongue—so many, in fact, that they could be gathered by the double handfuls. When the anteater thinks he has enough he removes his tongue quickly, putting it in his mouth, eating the ants and then going for more. In this way he eats all he wants or all he can catch with his tongue.

The flesh of this animal is filthy and has a very bad taste. In the beginning, however, the Christians encountered many hardships and trials in the new world and even tried to eat the anteater. But as soon as the Spaniards tasted this flesh they turned away from it.

The anthills have their entrance at the bottom, at the level of the ground, and it is so small that one could find it only with difficulty if one could not see ants entering and leaving. The anteater could not harm them through that opening; it is much easier to attack them through the cracks in the top of the mound, as I have explained.

## 21

## RABBITS AND HARES

In Tierra Firme there are both rabbits and hares. They are called this because in color of the back they resemble hares, but in other places they are white, on the belly as well as on the sides. Their legs are grayish brown. In fact, from what I have been able to learn, they are more like hares than rabbits, and they are smaller than the hares of Spain. Usually they are captured when the woods are burned over, and at times the Indians also catch them in traps.

## 22

## ARMADILLO

The armadillo[36] is a very strange animal to the Christians, and quite different from any animal in Spain or anywhere else. This animal is a quadruped. Its whole body and tail are covered with skin. Its hide is like the skin of a lizard, between white and gray, but somewhat more white. In appearance it is exactly like an armored horse, with its caparison and armor completely covering its body. From under the armor the tail comes out, and in their proper place the legs, and the neck and the ears in their place. In short, it is exactly like a warhorse with armor. This animal is about the size of a small

---

36. *Tatusia novemcincta.*

dog, or common cur dog, and is not vicious, but rather timid. They make their homes in mounds of earth, and by digging with their paws they hollow out their caves and burrows, somewhat like those made by rabbits. They are excellent food and are captured in nets, and some are killed by crossbowmen. Most often these animals are taken when the fields are burned over in preparation for planting or to renew the grass for cows and cattle.

I have eaten of them several times, and the flavor is better than that of kid. It is healthful food. I cannot help suspecting that this animal was known by those who first put horses in full trappings, for from the appearance of these animals they could have learned the form of the trappings for the armored horse.

### 23
### THE SLOTH

The sloth[37] is the stupidist animal that can be found in the world, and is so awkward and slow in movement that it would require a whole day to go fifty paces. The first Christians to see this animal, remembering that in Spain we are accustomed to call a Negro 'John White'—the saying to be taken in reverse—when they discovered this animal they gave it a reverse name, calling it 'swift' because it is very slow. This is a very strange animal and interesting to see in Tierra Firme, because it is so unlike any other animal. When full grown it is about two spans long, sometimes slightly longer. Many smaller ones are to be found, but they are young. They are a little narrower than they are long. They are quadrupeds, and on each small foot they have four long claws webbed together like those of a bird, but neither the claws nor the feet will support the animal. The legs are so small and the body so heavy, that the animal almost drags its belly along the ground. Its neck is tall and straight and equal like the handle of an engraver's tool, being the same size all along, and the head is no larger than the neck. At the end of the neck it has a face almost round, very much like that of an owl, and its hair makes a sort of outline of its almost round face, although it is a little longer than it

---

37. *Choloepus hoffmanni* or *Choloepus didactylus*.

is wide. Its eyes are small and round; its nose like that of a monkey. Its mouth is very small and it moves its neck from one side to another like a stupid thing. What it desires and wishes most is to grasp a tree or something which it can climb. Often these animals are captured in trees, in which they climb along very slowly, hanging upside down and holding on with their long claws. The coat of this animal is between white and gray, about the same color as the badger. It has no tail.

Its voice, heard only at night, is quite different from that of any other animal in the world. Throughout the night at regular intervals it can be heard singing six tones, one higher and louder than the next, and always in a descending order. The highest note is first, and from that it goes down the scale as one would sing *la, sol, fa, mi, re, ut*. So this animal sounds *ah, ah, ah, ah, ah, ah*. It certainly seems to me, as I said in the chapter on armadillos that such animals could have been the origin or suggestion of caparisoning a horse, so by hearing this animal sound its six notes the first inventor of music would have had the best suggestion in the world on which to base his scale. Because the sloth teaches us in his six tones the same thing that is heard in *la, sol, fa, mi, re, ut*.

But returning to my story, a short while after the animal makes this series of sounds, it repeats it again. It does this at night, and is never heard to sing during the day. For this reason as well as the fact that it has poor sight, I think it is a nocturnal animal and fond of darkness and shade.

Sometimes the Christians capture these animals and take them home and keep them. Even then the sloth will not move faster than they are ordinarily accustomed to move, even if they are threatened, struck, or prodded. If one comes to a tree, it will climb to the top branches and remain there eight or ten or twenty days. No one can find out what this animal eats. I had one in my home, and from my observations I have come to believe that this animal lives on air. There are many people in the New World who share this opinion, for the sloth has never been seen to eat anything, but it turns its head and mouth into the wind more often than in any other direction, from which one can see that it is very fond of air. It does not bite because its mouth is too small; nor is it poisonous. I have never seen such an ugly animal or one that is more useless.

## 24

## RACCOON

There are some small animals[38] resembling small gray dogs, with the snout and half the legs black. They have about the same form as young foxes in Spain, and are not less malicious, and bite very much. Some of these animals have been tamed, and they are very mischievous and cunning, much like monkeys. Their chief food, and the food they like best, is the crab. It is believed that they exist almost entirely on these. I had one of these animals, brought to me by a caravel of mine from the coast of Cartagena. It was given to our men there by the arrow-shooting Indians in exchange for two fishhooks. I kept it tied to a small chain a long time. They are very peaceful animals, and not as filthy as monkeys.

## 25

## MONKEYS

In the Indies there are so many different kinds of monkeys that they could not be described in a small space. There are many species and they play thousands of pranks. Every day some are brought to Spain, and so I shall say only a little about them.

Some of these monkeys are so clever that they imitate many of the things they see men do. There are many that as soon as they see an almond or pine kernel opened with a stone, they do the same thing, and they will open all that you give them if you place a stone where the animal can pick it up. Likewise they can throw a small stone, of the size and weight not too great for their strength, just as a man would throw it.

When the Christians go inland to make war upon some province, and pass through a forest in Tierra Firme where there are large black monkeys, the monkeys break the trunks and branches of the trees and hurl them at the Christians to break their heads. The Christians have to cover their heads with their shields and proceed cautiously, so they will not be injured and so none of their company will be wounded. Sometimes the stones which they throw at these monkeys lodge in

38. *Procyon cancrivorus.*

the tops of the trees. Then the monkeys hurl these down again upon the Christians. In this fashion a monkey threw one that had been thrown at him and struck one Francisco de Villacastur, servant of Governor Pedrarias de Avila, and this stone knocked out four or five of his teeth. I know this man, and I saw him several times before he received the blow from the stone thrown by the monkey, and he had his teeth. I have seen him many times since and without teeth, for he lost them as I have said.

When the Christians shoot arrows at the monkeys, or hit a monkey, the animals pull the arrows out and sometimes hurl them down again. Again, as soon as they pull out the arrow, they place it carefully in the branches of the trees so that it will not fall so that they may not be wounded by them again. Other monkeys break the arrows into small pieces.

Finally, there is so much to say about the pranks and the many different species of these monkeys that it would be difficult to believe without seeing them. Some of these animals are very small, about the size of a man's hand or even smaller; others are as large as a middle-sized mastiff. Between these two extremes there are monkeys of many different species, shapes, and colors, and very different one from the other.

## 26

## DOGS

In Tierra Firme the Carib arrow-shooting Indians have small cur dogs,[39] which they keep at home, and they are of all the colors of dogs in Spain. Some are shaggy, others smooth. They are mute and never bark, yelp, howl, nor do they whine or howl even if they are being killed by blows.

They look very much like small wolves, but they are not; they are true dogs. I have seen them killed without their making a sound. I have seen them in Darién, brought from the coast of Cartagena, from the land of the Caribs, where fishhooks had been traded for them. They never bark nor do anything except eat and drink. They are somewhat more shy than our dogs, except toward those in whose houses they live. They show deep affection toward those who feed them, and

---

39. *Canis familiaris.*

wag their tails and frisk about merrily, showing that they want to please the one who feeds them and the one they regard as master.

## 27
## OPOSSUM

The *churcha* [opossum][40] is a small animal, about the size of a small rabbit, of tawny color, very smooth hide, a pointed snout, and sharp fangs and teeth. Its long tail and ears are like a rat's. The opossums in Tierra Firme (like the marten in Castile) come to the houses at night to eat the chickens, or at least to cut their throats and suck the blood. For the latter reason they are more harmful, for if they should kill one hen and eat it to their fill they would do less damage. But it happens that they cut the throats of fifteen or twenty, or even more, if the chickens are not protected.

The unusual and strange thing about these animals is that if they have young at the time they make these nocturnal raids of killing chickens, they bring the young with them, placed in their breasts in this fashion: in the middle of the belly there is a pouch made of the animal's hide, just as one could form a pocket by joining two folds of a cape. The opening where the two folds of skin come together is somewhat tight so that the young can not fall out when the animal runs. Whenever she wishes, she can open the pouch and let the young out. Then the young walk on the ground, helping the mother suck blood from the hens she kills. And when the opossum thinks she has been heard and that someone with a light is coming to see what has frightened the chickens, the opossum instantly puts her young into the pouch and runs away if it is possible. But if her way is blocked, she climbs to the top of the house or henhouse to hide. Many times the opossum is captured alive; sometimes she is killed. What I have said has been observed many times, and the young have been found in the pouch, which contains the teats so the young can nurse while they ride along. I have seen some of these opossums and they have even killed my hens, as I have described. This animal has a bad odor, and it has skin, ears, and tail like a rat's. But it is much larger than a rat.

40. There are many species. This is probably *Didelphis aurita*.

Since I have written in detail concerning some animals, I want to inform your Majesty of what I remember of the birds I have seen in the New World. There are many birds of many different species and first I shall speak of those that are like our birds. Then I shall tell in detail what I remember about those that differ from those that are known in Spain.

## 28
## BIRDS SIMILAR TO THOSE IN SPAIN

In the Indies there are golden eagles[41] and black eagles, little eagles and light-colored eagles.[42] There are sparrow hawks and lanners, and merlins or duck hawks, except that they are blacker than those in Spain. There are kites that eat chickens and have the plumage and appearance of white eagles.[43]

There are other red-eyed birds larger than gerfalcons, and with very large talons. Their eyes are red, the plumage is very pretty and mottled like pretty goshawks that have moulted. They always go in pairs.

I knocked one down once from the top of a high tree with an arrow that struck him in the breast, and when he fell he was almost like a golden eagle, and was so well armed that it was a real treat to see his talons and his beak. He lived the rest of that day. I did not know what to call it, nor did any Spaniard who saw it. But the bird that this one most resembles, is the large goshawk,[44] but it is even larger than they. And so the Christians there call them goshawks. There are also ring doves and stock doves, and swallows, and quail, and martins, and purple herons, and night herons, and flamingos, except that the red color of the breast is much more vivid and the plumage much more beautiful than in the European flamingo. There are, too, cormorants, ducks, mallards, and wild geese, except that they are black as was said above. All these birds are migratory and are seen only at certain times. There are likewise owls and gulls.

---

41. *Aquila chrysaëtos.*
42. When Oveido describes American flora and fauna in such general terms, and when he describes in terms of European plants and animals, it is quite difficult, often impossible, to determine the exact American species referred to.
43. *Falco biarmicus.*
44. *Accipiter gentilis.*

## 29
## CONCERNING BIRDS OTHER THAN THOSE DESCRIBED ABOVE

There are so many different species of parrots that it would be a long task to describe them. They are better subjects for the painter's brush than for words. Since so many different species have been carried to Spain, it is hardly worth while to take time to describe them here.

A few days before the Catholic Sovereign Ferdinand passed from this existence, I carried to him in Placencia six arrow-shooting cannibal Carib Indians and six Indian girls, all handsome people. I also carried a sample of the sugar that was then beginning to be produced in Hispaniola at that time, and also several specimens of cassia fistula, of the first produced in that land by the Christians. I also presented to his Majesty thirty or more parrots representing ten or twelve different species. Most of them could speak very well. These parrots, although in Spain they seem to be slow, are strong flyers, and always go in pairs, male and female. They are very destructive to corn and other food crops cultivated by the Indians.

## 30
## MAN-OF-WAR BIRDS

There are large birds,[45] strong flyers, that most often fly very high. They are black and almost birds of prey. They have long slender wings, and the elbows of the wings are very sharp, and the tail is open, like that of the kite, so they call them fork-tails. They are larger than kites and have such confidence in their flight that many times ships sailing to the New World sight them twenty or thirty leagues or more out at sea, flying very high.

## 31
## TROPIC BIRDS

There are strong-flying white birds,[46] larger than ring doves, that have a long slender tail. For this reason they are

---

45. *Fregata magnificens.*
46. Of the three principal species, this is likely *Phaëton aethereus.*

called rush-tails. Although they are land birds, they are often seen far out at sea.

## 32

## BOOBY

There are some birds called crazy birds [boobies][47] that are smaller than gulls. Their feet are like those of ducks, and they settle on the water occasionally. When ships sail near those islands, about fifty or one hundred leagues away, and these birds see the ships, they fly to them, and when they are tired of flying, they light on the lateen yards and masts or main-topsails of the ships. These birds are so stupid and remain there so long that they are easily captured by hand. For this reason the sailors call them 'boobies.' These birds are black with gray heads and shoulders and have many feathers in proportion to the body. They are not good to eat, but sailors do eat them sometimes.

## 33

## PETREL

There are other very black birds[48] smaller than thrushes. I think it is one of the swiftest flying birds in the world. They fly at the level of the water, high or low as the waves may be. They are so extremely clever in rising or dropping with the water, flying close to the surface, that one could not believe it without seeing it. These birds have webbed feet as ducks and geese and are able to light on the water whenever they desire. Over almost the whole route from Spain to the Indies they are to be seen on the great Ocean Sea.

## 34

## NIGHTHAWK

In Tierra Firme there are some birds which the Christians call 'night birds.' They come out at sunset at the same time as the bats, with whom they have constant war, pursuing them and beating them. That is always a source of pleasure to those who observe it. There are many of these birds in Darién, and they are somewhat larger than swifts, and have the same kind

---

47. 'Pajaro bobo' is now 'penguin.' Obviously this is another bird. Alvarez López says it is *Sula fusca*.
48. *Hydrobates pelagicus*.

of wings and are as fast or faster in flight. Across the middle of each wing there is a band of white feathers. All the rest of its plumage is brown, almost black. These birds fly all night long, and at daybreak hide themselves and are not seen again until sunset, when they come out again to continue their customary feud with the bats.

### 35

### BATS

Since in the chapter above I spoke of the struggle between the nighthawks and bats, I must now say something about bats. There are many bats in Tierra Firme. They were very dangerous to Christians when first Vasco Núñez de Balboa and the bachelor Encisco went there at the time of the conquest of Darién. Although it was not known then, there is a simple and efficacious cure for the bite of the bat. At that time some Christians died of it and others were critically ill, but later the Indians taught them how to treat the bite.

Those bats are exactly like these in Spain but usually they bite at night, and most commonly they bite the tip of the nose or the tip of the fingers or toes, and suck such a great amount of blood from the wound that it is difficult to believe unless one has observed it. They have another peculiarity, and this is that if among one hundred men they bite one man, they will return to the same man on successive nights even though he be among a great number.

The remedy for this bite is to take a small amount of hot embers from the fire, as hot as can be tolerated, and place them on the wound. There is also another remedy: take water as hot as can be tolerated and wash the wound; then the bleeding stops and a cure is effected very shortly. The wound itself is small, for the bat takes out only a small circle of flesh. They have bitten me, and I have cured myself with hot water as I have described.

There are other bats in the island of St. John [Puerto Rico] that are eaten. They can be skinned very easily in scalding water. Then they appear like reed birds, very white, and fat and of good flavor, according to the Indians. Also some Christians have eaten them, especially those who are inclined to eat what they see others eat.

## 36

## TURKEYS

There are both light and dark turkeys with tails like those of Spanish turkeys.[49] In plumage some are golden with the belly and part of the breast white; others are black with the belly and part of the breast white. They both have on their heads a beautiful crest or panache, red feathers on the light one, black feathers on the black one. They are better to eat than Spanish turkeys. These turkeys are wild but can be domesticated if they are captured when young.

Since these birds are plentiful, many are killed by hunters. Some people say that the gobbler is light and the hen is black. Others are of the opposite opinion, saying that the gobbler is black while the hen is light. Others say that there are two species, that there are both male and female of each color. If the hunter does not hit the turkey in the head or in some other vulnerable spot, even if it is hit in a wing, it runs rapidly through the woods. Since the trees are very thick, the hunter must have a good fast dog or he will lose his labor and the game. One of these turkeys is worth a *ducado,* and at times even a *castellano,* or *peso* in gold, which has the same purchasing power as a *real* in Spain.

Other larger and more beautiful turkeys of better flavor have been found in New Spain. Many of these have been brought to the islands and to Castilla del Oro, and are raised domestically by the Christians. The females are ugly but the males handsome. Very often they spread their tails, but these are not so large or so pretty as the tails of Spanish turkeys. Nevertheless the rest of their plumage is very beautiful. Their heads and necks are covered with a skin without feathers, and this often changes its color when the bird is angry. Especially when they spread their tails it becomes very red. When they draw down their tails it becomes yellow and other colors, especially blackened, and sometimes it becomes a grayish-white. On his head, just above the beak, the turkey has a short erectile growth and when he spreads his tail this caruncle becomes longer or increases in length more than a span. From the middle of the breast there grows a cluster of bristles about the size of a finger, and those bristles, like a horse's tail, are

---

49. The Spanish 'turkey' is really the peacock.

very black and more than a span long. The flesh of these turkeys is very good and beyond all comparison better and more tender than the flesh of Spanish turkeys.

## 37
## PELICAN

There are birds in the Indies called pelicans[50] which are larger than large geese. Most of their plumage is brown, and in some parts yellow. They have a beak about two spans long, very wide near the head, gradually growing smaller toward the tip. They have a very large gular pouch. They are very much like a bird I saw in your Majesty's place in Brussels in Flanders. They call this bird 'hayna.'

I remember one day when your Majesty was dining in the large salon, they brought to your royal presence a large kettle of water containing live fish, and this bird ate them whole. I am of the opinion that that must have been a sea bird, for it had feet like those of a water bird or a goose. The pelican has that sort also, for they too are sea birds. In Panama, in 1521, I saw a man's coat placed in the pouch of a pelican. On the coast of Panama there are so many flocks of pelicans that they merit description. There are also many men in this capital of your Majesty's who have seen many times what I am about to describe.

Your Majesty knows, as I have already pointed out, that in Panama the tide of the South Sea rises and falls every six hours over a stretch of two leagues and more of land. At high tide the sea comes as close to the houses of Panama as the Mediterranean comes to the houses of Barcelona or Naples. The high tide brings many sardines—a marvelous thing—and one could not believe there would be such an abundance of sardines without seeing them. The chief of that land, when I was there, every day was obligated and ordered by your Majesty's governor to bring usually three dugouts or boats filled with these sardines, and to empty them out in the public square. This he did day after day, and one of the councilmen of the city without charge divided these fish among the Christians. There would have been enough of those fish to sustain many

---

50. *Pelecanus occidentalis.* Oviedo uses the word *alcatraz*, which is really the gannet (*Sula bassana*).

more people, a population even larger than the city of Toledo, and even if they had nothing more to eat, the large numbers of sardines would have been more than enough to sustain them.

The pelicans appeared always at high tide with the sardines, so many of them flying over the water that they filled the air. They would always dive into the water, catch as many sardines as they could, then rise from the water again. After gobbling down the fish, they would dive into the sea again, then rise again without ever resting. When the tide goes out, the pelicans go with it, continuing their fishing as I have described. Along with the pelicans come the frigate birds, described above. As soon as a pelican rises with the fish it has caught, the frigate bird beats it and pursues it so closely that it casts up the fish it has swallowed. As soon as a fish is thrown out, the frigate bird catches it before it falls into the water. It is a pleasure to watch this game that goes on every day.

There are so many of these pelicans that the Christians send dugouts and boats to islands and reefs near Panama to get young pelicans that are not old enough to fly. They kill as many as they want with sticks and fill their dugouts with them. They are fat and good to eat. The adults are not good to eat but they are taken for their fat, which is made into very good oil for burning in lamps. This oil gives a gentle light which burns very beautifully. In this manner and for this reason many pelicans are slaughtered, and yet it always seems that the number that can be seen fishing for sardines is on the increase.

38

## CORMORANT

Further back I said that there are cormorants[51] of the same species as those in Spain. I shall not describe them here, but tell you of the great number to be found on the South Sea on the coast of Panama. At times so many come in search of sardines, which I have described in the previous chapter, that when they light on the water they cover a great part of it, and the flock is almost as large as the plain stretching away from this city of Toledo. These flocks or multitudes of cormorants are seen every day in many places on the South Coast. Those that rest on the water appear to be a piece of velvet or black

---

51. *Phalacrocorax carbo* or *Phalacrocorax graculus*.

cloth without a break, so close are these birds one to another. Like the pelicans they come and go with the tide, fishing for sardines.

Some people like these sardines, but I do not. They are so sweet that each of the three times I have eaten them I have become ill. No fish I have ever eaten in Spain or in the New World is quite so abominable. But other men find them quite good.

## 39
## BLACK VULTURE

There are many Spanish chickens there and they are increasing rapidly, because a hen always hatches as many eggs as she can cover with her wings. These birds have been propagated from those that were carried there earlier. But there are also wild chickens that are as large as turkeys. They are black, with the head and part of the neck somewhat gray, or at least not as black as the other parts. But that gray or less black part is not feathers but skin.[52]

They have poor flesh and a worse taste, are very gluttonous, and eat much filth, dead Indians and animals. They smell like musk. The odor is very pleasing as long as they are alive, but it is lost as soon as the birds are killed. They are good for nothing except to provide feathers for arrows and darts. They can stand a hard blow, and the bolt that kills one must have tremendous force or hit its head or break a wing. They are very troublesome, and like to stay in or near the city in order to be able to eat the garbage.

## 40
## PARTRIDGE

In Tierra Firme 'partridges'[53] are as good as those in Spain, and just as tasty. They are as large as the chickens of Castile, and have very large breasts. They have so much flesh that only a very heavy eater could consume one at one meal. The feathers are tan on the breast as well as on the wings and neck, the rest is of the same color as the shoulders of our Spanish partridges. The eggs laid by these partridges are almost round and

---

52. This is the *zopilote*, 'black vulture' (*Catharista atratus*).
53. These 'partridges' must be the tinamou of Central and South America, the chief genera being *Crypturus*, *Tinamus*, and *Rhynchotus*.

not oval like hen eggs. They are almost as large as hen eggs, and are a beautiful turquoise blue. The Indians catch these birds with bird calls, and by setting traps for them. I have taken some of these alive, and I have eaten them several times in Tierra Firme. They are caught as follows: the Indian catches a lock of hair above his forehead almost on the crown of his head, and pulls it and then loosens it, shaking his head from side to side, and with his mouth he makes a whistling sound like that made by partridges. The birds are attracted by this call and fall into the traps made of henequen fibre, which was described above in chapter ten. These birds are good when baked, but first they are broiled slightly. In this way or boiled or cooked in any other way, they are very good. They taste much like Spanish partridges. The flesh is quite firm, and they are better eaten on the second day after they have been killed, because then they are more high and tender.

There is also a small species similar to our gray partridges,[54] and they are quite good to eat. This small species, however, does not taste so much like our Spanish partridges as do the large species described above. They are grayish in color, some being very light. They are more easily caught than the large ones and are better for sick people, since they are not so hard to digest.

## 41

## PHEASANT

The pheasants of Tierra Firme do not have the same plumage as those in Spain, nor are they so beautiful. They have an excellent flavor, and taste much like the large partridges which were discussed in the preceding chapter. The plumage is brown almost like that of the partridges. They are not as large, but they stand higher, and have long wide tails. Many are killed with crossbows. They have a certain call that sounds like a whistle, quite different from the call of the partridge and much louder, for they can be heard a great distance, and there is a long interval between calls. Because of this the bowmen kill them with ease.

---

54. The small 'partridge' must be of the genus *Ortyx*, or the closely related *Eupsychortyx* or *Odontophorus*.

## 42

## TOUCAN

There is in Tierra Firme a bird that the Christians call *picudo* ['big bill,' toucan] because it has a small body and large beak. The beak weighs more than the whole body. This bird is only slightly larger than a quail, but it appears much larger because of its beautiful thick varicolored plumage. Its turned-down beak is as much as six inches long. At the head the beak is about three finger-breadths wide. The bird's tongue is a feather, and it can whistle loudly. With its beak it makes holes in trees, where it nests and raises its young. It is a very strange bird, and different from any other that I have seen because of its feather tongue, its appearance, and its disproportionately large bill. No bird can so securely and safely protect its young from cats. Because of the location of the nest, cats cannot enter the hole in the tree to take the eggs or young birds. When the birds hear a cat they get into the nest and turn their bills out, and give the cat such pecks that the cat deems it wise not to molest the young birds.

## 43

## 'CRAZY BIRD'

There are some birds which the Christians call 'crazy birds'[55] in order to give them a name opposite to their characteristics, which is sometimes done, as was explained above. Really no bird that I have seen in the New World is more wise and instinctively cunning in raising its young and protecting them from danger. These birds are small and almost black, somewhat larger than thrushes of Spain. They have a few white feathers on their necks, and are as active as magpies. Very rarely do they light on the ground, and they build their nests in vacant trees and solitary trees separated some distance from each other, because monkeys usually swing and leap from one tree to another and do not descend to the ground through fear of other animals. If they are thirsty they descend to drink when they know they will not be attacked. Therefore these birds do not try to raise their young except in solitary trees.

55. José Miranda says (p. 182) that the 'crazy bird' (*pájaro loco*) is the 'oropéndola,' a name sometimes given to the *zanate* (*Quiscalus macrourus*).

They build a bag-shaped nest about as long as a man's arm. At the bottom the nest is wide, gradually becoming smaller at the top where it is attached to the tree, where there is a hole through which the birds enter. This opening is barely large enough to permit the bird to enter the nest.

If cats should climb the trees where these nests are hung, they are not able to eat the birds. The twigs and straw and other things with which these cunning birds build their nests are rough and thorny so that a cat cannot touch them without injuring himself. The nests are so closely woven and strong that no man could copy them. If the cat tries to put his paw through the opening of the nest to take out the eggs or the small birds, he cannot reach them since the nest is three or four spans deep and the cat's paw will not reach to the bottom.

These birds build many of these nests on one tree, for one or two reasons: because they are by nature very sociable and like to live with members of their own species, like martins, or if by chance a cat should climb the tree where the birds are nesting there is such a large number of nests that it is difficult for the cat to determine which he shall attack, and there is such a large number of adult birds that fly around, and when they see the cats, they give warning.

## 44

## MAGPIES

In Tierra Firme and also on the islands there are magpies that are smaller than those in Spain. They have the same activity and manner of jumping along. But they are entirely black, and have black bills shaped like those of the parrot. These birds have long tails and are somewhat larger than thrushes.

## 45

## GOLDFINCH

There are birds called goldfinches,[56] and they are very small, like those here that are called *pinchicos* or 'bird of seven

---

56. Oviedo's comparison here is with the European goldfinch (*Carduelis carduelis*) known in Spain as *pintadillo, colorín, soldadito.* A number of New World birds are called 'seven colors,' the *Tanagra bonaerensis* of La Plata and *Cyanospiza ciris* of Mexico.

69

colors.' These small birds are afraid of cats and always nest along the banks of the river or the seashore, where the branches of the trees that hold the nests will bend down to the water if a light weight is placed on the branches. They build their nests almost on the tips of the branches, and when a cat climbs out on the branch it bends down to the water. The cat, afraid of falling into the water, then turns back from the nest for fear he will fall. Of all the animals in the world none surpasses the cat in slyness. And even though most animals can swim, these cats do not, and drown very easily. These birds build their nests in such a fashion that even though they become saturated and filled with water, the water runs out immediately. And even though small birds, however young they may be, are in the nest that goes under the water, they are not drowned.

## 46

### NIGHTINGALES AND OTHER SONG BIRDS

There are many nightingales[57] and other songbirds that sing beautifully and melodiously in many different manners. They are also of many colors. Some are solid yellow; others are red, of such fine and excellent color that one could not imagine it except in a ruby. There are some of many colors, some of few, and others of only one color. They are much more beautiful than the song birds in Spain, Italy, or any other of the many other provinces or lands that I have seen. Many of them are caught in traps and cages, with birdlime and in other ways.

## 47

### HUMMINGBIRD

There are some little birds so small that they are no larger than the end of the thumb. Stripped of feathers they are only half that size. Not only is this bird exceptionally small, but it is so swift in flight that it is as impossible to see its wings as it is those of a beetle or a bumblebee. There is no person who

---

57. Certainly these birds are not nightingales, and this meager description makes positive identification impossible. Here Oviedo probably is referring to the mockingbird, a subspecies of *Mimus polyglottos*.

sees it fly but that thinks it is a bumblebee. They build very small nests. I saw one of these birds and its nest in the pan of a balance for weighing gold, and together they weighed only two *tomines* which is equal to twenty-four grains, feathers and all. Without its feathers it would have weighed much less. They are so small that they look like the little birds placed by illuminators in the margins of books of hours. Their plumage is very beautiful; they are gold, green, and of other colors. Its bill is as long as its body, and as slender as a pin. They are very bold, and if a man climbs a tree where they are nesting, the bird attacks his eyes and darts away and returns to the attack with incredible speed. This bird is so small that I would not speak of it if there were not other eyewitnesses here in your Majesty's court. They make their nests of small tufts of cotton, which is found there in abundance.

## 48
## MIGRATION OF BIRDS

Some years in the month of March I have seen over a space of fifteen or twenty days, and in some years over a longer period, the sky covered with birds from morning to night, flying so high that some of them were almost out of sight, others flying lower but still high above the hills and mountains. They fly from north to south. They come from the sea toward the land and cover the whole sky from north to south and a wide section east to west. Apparently most of these birds are golden eagles and many large species and other birds of prey. One cannot distinguish the differences and the color of the plumage because they fly too high for this to be discerned by the naked eye. But from their manner of flying and the difference in sizes one can see they are of many different species. This flyway of the birds is above the city and province of Santa María del Antigua del Darién, in Tierra Firme, in that part that is called Castilla del Oro.

There are so many other species of birds in Tierra Firme that it would be too laborious to describe them all in detail. I do not remember any others at present. Since I have described many others in my *General History of the Indies*, I include here only descriptions of those fresh in my memory.

## 49
## FLIES, MOSQUITOES, BEES, WASPS, ANTS, AND SIMILAR INSECTS

In the West Indies and in Tierra Firme there are very small flies. Rarely does one see there the flies we have in Europe. There are many kinds of annoying mosquitoes, especially in some areas along the coast and rivers. Many places inland are free of them. There are many dangerous, poisonous wasps, whose sting is beyond comparison worse than the sting of Spanish wasps. They have about the same color of those in Spain, but they are larger and of a somewhat brighter yellow. Their wings are black, tipped with tan. They build very large nests, and their racemes, filled with cells, are as big as the honeycomb made by bees in Spain. But the nests are grayish white and dry, containing no liquid. The young or whatever the larvae feed on are contained therein. They build many of these nests in trees and also in the roofs and timbers of houses.

## 50
## BEES

There are many small bees about the size of flies, that breed in hollow trees. The tips of their wings are cut across in the same manner as the points of Victorian machetes. Across the middle of the wing there is a white bar. They do not sting or do harm. In fact, they have no stinger. They make large honeycombs. The little holes through which they enter are four times as large as those made by the Spanish bees, even though the bees are smaller. The honey is good and wholesome, but it is almost as dark as boiled honey.

## 51
## ANTS

There are very many different kinds of ants, and some are unbelievably destructive. They have inflicted great damage on trees, canefields, and other things necessary to man. Those eaten by the anteater are small and black. There are others that are red, and others that are called *comején* [termite], one half ant, the other half a small worm in a small white case which drags behind. They are very harmful and penetrate timbers and houses. These termites do much damage. If they go up a tree or wall, or wherever they make their track, they build a tunnel of earth about as thick as a finger. Through that tunnel or covered track they go to wherever they want to settle, and where they stop they enlarge the tunnel greatly, making a house of clay three or four spans long and just as wide.

There they raise their young and cause the wood to rot and they eat it away until the walls are as hollow as a honeycomb. It is necessary to keep on the lookout for them and to destroy their runs and houses as soon as they are discovered, before they have time to damage the houses. To that animal a house is the same as cloth to a moth.

There are other larger ants and in many species. The worst are black ants almost as large as bees. They are very pestiferous. From them and other poisonous ingredients the Indians make the poison with which they tip their arrows. There is no antidote for this poison and of those wounded by it, not four in one hundred recover. We have seen many Spaniards bitten by these ants and immediately they developed a high fever, followed by great swelling of the body.

Other ants are the same size as the common ants in Spain. But those in Spain are red, while these and all the others I have described above in Tierra Firme are dark.

## 52

### HORSEFLY

In Tierra Firme there are many annoying horseflies that have a terrible bite. There are so many species and in such large numbers that the reader would be bored by a detailed description.

## 53

### WINGED ANTS

In those regions there are winged ants, like those in Spain. They are formed when the ants sprout wings, and are somewhat smaller than our flying ants.

## 54
## PIT VIPERS

In Castilla de Oro, of Tierra Firme, there are many vipers[58] like those in Spain, and persons who are bitten by them soon die. Few live beyond the fourth day if they are not helped. There is one species smaller than the others with a blunt tail that can spring into the air and bite a man. Therefore some people call these snakes 'springers.' Their bite is poisonous and ordinarily fatal. One of these bit one of my Indian servant girls who was working in a house on one of my estates, and she was immediately treated with many things, including bleeding or making two lancet incisions in the foot on which she was bitten. In spite of the fact that we did for her everything the surgeons ordered, nothing was of any avail. They could not draw a drop of blood out of her foot, only a yellow fluid. Nothing helped her, and she died before the third day. The same thing has happened to other people. This Indian girl who died was about fourteen years old or less and she spoke Spanish as well as if she had been born and bred in Castile. She said that the snake that bit her on the instep was about two spans long, and that it sprang through the air more than six paces to strike her. Many people who know these snakes corroborate this statement and say they have seen other people die from these bites, for these snakes are the most poisonous of that land.

## 55
## SNAKES AND SERPENTS

I have seen slender snakes seven or eight feet long in Tierra Firme. They are so red that at night they look like live coals, and during the day they are as red as blood.[59] They are poisonous, but not so much so as the vipers.

There are other smaller black snakes that come out of the rivers and crawl on land. They too are poisonous.

There are other brown poisonous snakes that are somewhat larger than the fer-de-lance.

---

58. Oviedo is speaking of snakes of the family *Crotalidae*. The species seen by Oviedo may have been the fer-de-lance (*Bothrops atrox*) or the bushmaster (*Lachesis mutus*), Alvarez López, p. 213. The description of the snake's ability to spring 'more than six paces' is at least epic in exaggeration.
59. *Elaps corallinus*. (Alvarez López, p. 213.)

There are other very long spotted snakes.[60] I saw one of these in 1515 on the island Hispaniola, near the coast at the foot of the Pedernales mountains. I measured it and it was more than twenty feet long, and thicker than a man's fist at its thickest part. It must have been killed that day since it did not stink and the blood was fresh and it bore three or four sword slashes. These snakes are not as poisonous as those described above, but they are so large that one is terrified to look at them.

I remember that in 1522 when I was in Darién in Tierra Firme, a certain Pedro de la Calleja, a native of Colindres, one league from Laredo, an honorable man and a gentleman, came from the fields very frightened. He said that he had seen in a path running through a corn field only the head and part of the body of a snake or serpent. He could not see the whole length of body because the corn was very thick. He swore the snake's head was larger than the bent knee of a medium-sized man, and that its eyes seemed no smaller than those of a large calf. Seeing it, he did not dare go on, but turned back. He told this to me and to many others, and we believed it, because many people who heard the story had seen snakes like the one described by Pedro de la Calleja.

A few days later one of my servants, Francisco Rao, native of Madrid, killed a snake that was twenty-two feet long, and at its largest part it was thicker than a man's two fists. Most of the people in the town saw it.

## 56

## IGUANA

The iguana is a sort of quadruped serpent, very frightful to look at but good to eat. This animal or serpent, described in chapter six, is found in great numbers on the island and in Tierra Firme.

## 57

## LIZARDS OR DRAGONS

There are many lizards similar to those in Spain, but they are not poisonous. There are others twelve or fifteen feet long

---

60. Boa constrictor or the anaconda.

or longer,[61] and thicker than a chest. Some of the big ones are almost as thick as a barrel, with head and other parts of the body in proportion. They have a long snout, with the upper lip pierced by the tusks, which are in the lower part of the mouth. They have fierce-looking teeth and tusks. In the water they are very swift, but on land slow and awkward when compared to their agility in the water. Many of them live along the sea coast, and they enter and leave the sea by the rivers and streams that flow into the sea. They have four feet and a very strong shell. The middle of the back is studded with bony knobs from head to tail. The skin is so tough that no sword or lance can pierce it. These lizards or dragons can be wounded only in the sides and belly because there the flesh is soft and vulnerable.

In the month of December, in the driest part of the year, when the rivers do not overflow their banks and when there are no rains, these animals lay their eggs, so they will not be washed away by freshets. They go to the sandy beaches or river banks and make a hole in the sand and deposit two hundred or three hundred or more eggs. The eggs are covered with sand and after the time of incubation they are hatched by the sun, and the young come out from under the sand and make their way to the river that is nearby. They are no longer than a span, but later they grow to be as large as I have described above.

In some places these animals are so numerous that they present a terrifying spectacle. For the most part they inhabit the pools and lagoons of rivers, and when they come out on the land and shore the whole area smells of musk. Often they come out to sleep on the sand near the water. When they wander farther away and Christians come upon them, they flee to the water. They cannot run in curves, or from one side to another, only in a straight line. So if one chases a man, he will not catch him provided the man knows this and turns back in his flight. In this way these animals have been beaten and stabbed to death or forced to return to the water. It is best, however, to shoot them with guns or crossbows from a distance for with other arms, such as swords, darts, and lances, one can inflict small damage unless one strikes the animal in the belly or soft sides, because there

61. Alligators; *Crocodylus acutus*.

they are quite vulnerable. When they run on land they arch their tails over their backs, like a cock's tail, and the belly does not drag the ground but is held up a span or more according to the length of the animal's legs. They have strong legs and feet and long claws. Really these lizards are very fierce to behold.

Some people say they are crocodiles but this is not true. The crocodile does not have any means of breathing except through the mouth, but these lizards or dragons do. And the crocodile has two jaws, and can move the upper as well as the lower jaw. These lizards can move only the lower jaw. In the water they are very swift and very dangerous, and often eat men, dogs, horses, and cows that ford the streams. Knowing this, men who ford streams infested by them always cross at the rapids where the water is shallow and the current swift. The lizards never go where the water is shallow and swift.

Often when one is killed, there will be found in his belly one or two basketfuls of round stones, which the lizard eats for pleasure and digests, too. Very often they are caught on big hooks fastened to chains, and sometimes they are surprised out of the water and shot.

I think these are sea animals and not land animals, even though they are hatched from eggs on land, as I have said. The eggs from which they are hatched are as large, or larger, than goose eggs, and are as large at one end as at the other. If you drop one on the ground it does not break. Only the outside shell, about like that of a goose egg, breaks. Between the outside shell and the white there is a thin membrane that looks like parchment, which can be broken only by an iron point or a sharp stick. If you drop one of these softshelled eggs upon the ground it will bounce as if it were an inflated ball.

These eggs have no yolks, they are all whites, and when cooked in an omelet they are very tasty. On several occasions I have eaten the eggs but I have never tasted the flesh of the lizards. At the beginning of the conquest many Christians ate them, especially the little ones, and liked them. When a Christian would find these eggs in the sand, he would carry the whole nest of them to Darién, and receive five or six *castellanos* or more according to the number of eggs. Ordinarily he would receive one silver *real* for each egg. I have paid that price for them and often ate them in 1514. But later, when food and cattle came to be more abundant, the men ceased searching for these eggs. However, if they should find them, they still eat them.

## 58

## SCORPION

There are poisonous scorpions[62] in many parts of Tierra Firme. I have found them at Santa Marta, three leagues inland from the port where the Armada sent by his Majesty Ferdinand V, God rest his soul, touched in 1514. They are almost black on a lighter color. Many times I have seen them in Panama on the coast of the South Sea.

## 59

## SPIDERS

There are some spiders larger than a man's spread-out hand. I saw the body of a spider, exclusive of the legs, that was as large as a sparrow. It was covered with down. The color was dark brown, and the eyes larger than those of a sparrow. These large spiders are poisonous, but I have seen very few of them. There are many others larger than our Spanish spiders.

## 60

## CRABS

Crabs are land animals that come from holes they make in the earth. The head and body are entirely round and in some measure resemble a falcon's hood. Four feet come from each side, and two mouths, like pincers, one larger than the other, with which they bite. The bite is very painful but is not poisonous. Its shell or body is smooth and thin like the shell of an egg except that it is harder. The color is gray or white or bluish purple. They walk sideways and are good to eat. The Indians are very fond of them, and in Tierra Firme there

---

62. Oviedo could have seen many species of scorpion. He was most likely to encounter *Opistacanthus lepturus*.

are many crabs, and there are many Christians who like them. Crabs are inexpensive and tasty. When Christians go inland this is food readily available, and very good when roasted over coals. Finally, the form of the crab is about the same as we depict the sign of Cancer.

In Andalusia, on the seacoast and on the banks of the Guadalquivir where it enters the Atlantic ocean at San Lúcar, and in many other places, there are many crabs, but they are water crabs. Those I speak of here are land crabs. Sometimes those of the Indies are harmful, and those who eat them die, especially if the crabs have eaten poisonous things or manchineel apples, which will be described later, from which the Carib Indians make poison for their arrows. Christians protect themselves by not eating the crabs which are found near manchineel trees. Even if one eats many of these good crabs, they will not hurt one and it is not food that causes indigestion.

## 61

## TOADS

There is an offensively large number of nonpoisonous toads in Tierra Firme. The greatest number that I have seen was in the city of Darién. They were so large that when they died during the dry season such large bones remained, especially the ribs, that they looked like the bones of a cat or some other animal about that size. As the waters go down, the toads gradually disappear until the following year, when they reappear with the rains. There are not so many now as there used to be. The reason is that the land is being drained and cultivated by Spaniards, and many trees and forests are being cleared, and with the breeding of cows, mares, and cattle the land is being dried up and each day it is becoming more healthful and beautiful.

These toads sing in three or four ways, and not one is pleasing. Some sing like those here in Spain, others whistle, and others make still different sounds. Some of these toads are green, some are gray, and others are almost black. But they are all ugly, large, and annoying—since there are so many. As I have said, they are not poisonous. Wherever precautions are taken against water damming up, and when the water flows freely or is used up, there are no toads. Then they go in search of swamps.

## THE TREES, PLANTS, AND HERBS OF THE INDIES, ISLANDS, AND TIERRA FIRME

Since we have already spoken of the trees that have been carried from Spain—and they all grow well there—I want to speak of the trees native to the Indies. All of the many species that grow on the islands, as well as many more, also grow in Tierra Firme. I shall describe those that I remember, keeping in mind, however, what I said at the beginning of this document, that all I say here, and other things I may have forgotten, I have described fully in my *General History of the Indies*.

### 62

### MAMMEE

The principal food plants of the Indians are yuca and Indian corn, from which bread is made. A fermented drink, already described, is also made from corn. There is a fruit called mammee[63] which grows on a large tree with beautiful cool leaves. The fruit is handsome and excellent, of a very delicate flavor and at its thickest part the size of two fists placed together. In color it is very much like the wild pear, the rind tawny but more firm and thick than that of the wild pear. The stone is in three parts, close together and in its center, like seeds, and about the color and texture of peeled grafted chestnuts, and they really could be mistaken for chestnuts if they had the same flavor. But that three-part stone or seed is as bitter as gall. The seed is covered by a very thin membrane, and between this membrane and the rind there is tawny colored pulp which tastes like peaches or even better, and is of very pleasant odor. This fruit is firmer and much better in taste than peaches. The flesh between the seed and the rind is about as thick as a finger or a little less, and you could not find better fruit.

### 63

### SOURSOP

The soursop[64] is a large and tall beautiful tree with straight branches and long wide green leaves. It bears cones, or fruit that resembles them, as large as melons but longish in shape.

63. *Mammea americana.*
64. *Annona muricata.*

On top the fruit has certain decorations that look like scales but are not, nor can they be removed. It is covered all over with a rind as thick as a melon rind. Inside it is filled with a white pulp that, although firm, is juicy and of a delicate taste that is somewhat sharp and pleasant. The flesh contains seeds larger than those of the drumstick tree, which are of the same color and almost as hard. Even if a man eats a soursop that weighs two or three pounds or more it will not hurt his stomach or give him indigestion, for this is beautiful and excellent fruit. One can eat everything except the thin rind and the seeds. Some of these weigh four pounds or more. Even if one is broken open, the flesh remains edible for several days, although it tends to become dry and shrinks since the juice and liquid drop from it, and ants are attracted to the open part. Consequently once a soursop is opened, it is all eaten. There are many of these soursop trees on the islands as well as in Tierra Firme.

## 64

## GUAVA

The guava tree[65] is very pretty, with leaves resembling those of the black mulberry tree except that they are smaller. When it is in bloom it is very fragrant, especially the flower of a certain species of this tree. It bears apple-like fruit larger than our apples, and heavier even if they were of the same size. They have many seeds, or rather they are filled with small hard granules, but these are bothersome only to those who eat the fruit for the first time. Those who know this fruit think it is very delicious and like it better than apples. Inside some are red, others white. The best that I have found were in the vicinity of Darién and in certain parts of Tierra Firme. Those of the islands are not so good.

## 65

## COCONUT

The coconut[66] is a species of palm, in size and leaf resembling the royal date palm. They differ, however, as to the growth of leaves, since those of the coconut spring from the

65. *Psidium guajaba.*
66. *Cocos nucifera.*

trunk like the fingers of both hands that have been intertwined. So the leaves are alternate. These palms or coconut trees are very tall and there are many of them on the coast of the South Sea in the province of cacique Chiman, whom I once held with two hundred Indians as a part of my property. These palms produce a fruit called coconuts. As it grows on the tree, the fruit is larger than a man's head. From the outside to the center, where the fruit is found, it is covered with layers of fibre like that on the palmettos of Andalusia. I call them palmettos because they are not tall palms.

The Indians in the East Indies can make very good cloth and cords from that fibre. They make the cloth in three or four forms, for sails as well as for clothes. The cords are both large and small, some being large enough to be used as ropes and cables on ships. In your Majesty's Indies, however, the natives do not use cords and cloth made of the coconut fibre as much as they do in the East because they have an abundance of very good cotton.

The fruit that is in the above-described fibrous husk is as large as a man's fist, some as large as two, more or less. It is a sort of round, hard nut, somewhat oval in shape. The shell is about one eighth of an inch thick, and inside, adhering to the inside of the shell of the nut is a layer of white meat half as thick as a man's little finger, as white as a peeled almond and of a better taste than almonds and of excellent flavor. They are eaten as one eats peeled almonds. After the fruit is chewed there remains a husk as in the case of the almond, and if you swallow it, it is not bad. When one has swallowed the juice, before the husk or covering is swallowed, it seems that the part that remains in the mouth is somewhat rough, but that is not so, and it is not necessary to spit it out, especially if the coconut is fresh and has been plucked from the tree recently. Instead of eating it, if one pounds the meat of the coconut and strains it, one gets milk which is much better and sweeter than cow's milk, and of good quality. The Christians pour it into the meal that they make of corn, making something like porridge. Coconut milk mixed with the porridge makes a good dish. It does not give one indigestion and it gives the same pleasure and satisfies hunger in such fashion that it makes one feel that one has eaten a very fine meal.

In the center of this fruit, surrounded by the meat, is a

hollow filled with a clear and excellent liquid. There is about the amount that one egg would contain, more or less, according to the size of the coconut. This liquid is the most nourishing, the most excellent, the most palatable thing that one can imagine or drink, and as soon as one has swallowed it there is no part of man—de planta pedis usque ad verticem[67]—that does not have a perfect feeling of well-being and marvelous contentment. Certainly it has the most palatable taste of all things one can find on earth and I cannot praise it highly enough. After removing the meat, the natives often make vessels of the coconut shells. The shells are smoothed and polished until they become a brownish-black color. Persons who have kidney colic receive marvelous relief if they drink from these vessels, for this causes the stone to be broken up and expelled with the urine.

This fruit is called coconut[68] for this reason: when pulled from the tree the fruit shows a small cavity at the place where the stem was attached, and above it there are two other natural cavities. The fruit looks like a monkey that wheedles or flirts. But in fact this tree is a species of palm, and according to Pliny and other naturalists all palms are efficacious in treating kidney diseases. From this comes the idea that the coconut, as the fruit of the palm trees, is also good for such illnesses.

## 66

## PALMS

In the chapter above we said that coconuts are a species of palms, and therefore we should not continue further with descriptions of other trees until we have said something about palms. Up to now no date palms have been found in that new land. But due to the diligence of the Christians, these palms are now found in the islands of Santo Domingo or Hispaniola, and also Cuba, San Juan, and Jamaica, in the yards of private homes as well as in orchards and gardens. These have grown from the seeds of dates carried there from the old world. There are some very beautiful ones at many houses in Santo Domingo. At my home in that city there is a palm that bears much fruit

---

67. From head to foot.
68. The Spanish word *coco* means 'face,' 'grimace;' *cocar* means 'to make a face, grimace; to flirt.'

every year; it is very large and one of the most beautiful palm trees in that land.

There are seven or eight different species of palms that are native to the islands and to Tierra Firme. There is one that has leaves like the palmettos of Andalusia, the leaves being about the size of a man's extended hand. The fruit of these trees is a small round berry. There are other palms that have leaves like those of the date palm, and produce larger berries, but not so hard as those of the tree mentioned above. There is another palm with the same kind of leaves, and the little palm sprouts are very good to eat. These also bear berries. Still another species, somewhat lower and thicker than the one described above, has sprouts that can be eaten. It also bears berries.

There are other tall palms with very good sprouts. These palms bear coconuts no larger than Cordovan olives. They are like coconuts without the outside tow husk, having only the shell with the three little holes which make it look like a wheedling, pouting monkey. But these coconuts are small and solid and therefore worthless.

There are other tall spiny palms[69] of most excellent wood, which is black, hard, and heavy, and takes a beautiful polish. The wood is so heavy that it will not float on water, but sinks to the bottom at once. Very good arrows and darts are made of this wood, and even lances and piques. I say piques because on the south coast near Esquegna and Urraca, the Indians have very beautiful long pikes made of this wood. And when the Indians fight with long darts which they throw, they make them of this wood. They are as long as light lances, with very sharp points. These will penetrate both a man and his shield. The Indians also make clubs to fight with, and any shaft or anything else made of this wood is very beautiful. For cymbals or guitars, or any other wooden musical instrument, this wood is excellent, because in addition to being very hard, it is black as jet.

## 67
## PINES

On the island Hispaniola there are native pines[70] like those

---

69. R. M. Moscoso, *Catalogus Florae Domingensis*, p. xix, says this is *Roystonea regia*.
70. This is the *Pinus occidentalis*. See Alvarez López, p. 271.

of Spain, which do not bear pine nuts. I cannot remember having seen these pine trees on other islands or in Tierra Firme.

## 68
## EVERGREEN OAK

On the coast of the South sea, towards the west after one leaves Panama and before reaching the province of Esquegna, there are many evergreen oaks. They bear acorns that are good to eat. I have also verified that there are many of these trees in Tierra Firme from the Spaniards who have been there and have eaten of the acorns.[71]

## 69
## VINES AND GRAPES

In the wooded parts of Tierra Firme there are many good wild vines covered with grapes,[72] some bearing single grapes, others in bunches. They are larger, better, and not so sour as those that grow in the groves in Spain. I have eaten them many times and in large quantities. I want to make it clear that grapes and vines would do well there. All of these grapes that I have seen and eaten are black. In Santo Domingo I have eaten very good large white grapes grown on vines on arbors from vine shoots brought from Spain. They are as good as those grown in Spain.

## 70
## PAPAYA

On the west coast, going from the town of Acla and passing on by the gulf of San Blas, and the port of Nombre de Dios, down the coast, in the land of Veragua and on the islands of Corobaro, there are very tall big trees,[73] with very large leaves and much larger than Spanish fig trees. They bear 'figs' [papaya] as large as small melons, and these grow close to the trunk and at the top and in great profusion. They have a thin skin and all the rest is thick flesh like that of the melon and it

---

71. Alvarez López points out (p. 217) that this could be any of several species of *Quercus*, although none is properly an *encina* (evergreen oak). It is not the *Q. ilex* of southern Europe and may not even be *Q. virens*.
72. There are many species of grapes in America. This is probably the *Vitis quinquefolia* (Alvarez López, p. 217).
73. *Carica papaya*.

is very tasty. They are cut in slices like melons. In the middle of the 'fig,' or this fruit, there are small black seeds encased in a sort of membrane like those of a quince. There would be about enough to fill a hen's egg, more or less, according to the size of the fruit. These seeds are also eaten, since they are good and have the very same flavor as peppergrass. Therefore those of us who serve your Majesty in that land call them 'peppergrass figs.' And those seeds have been planted in Darién, and they produced good fig trees. I have eaten many of these 'figs' and they are just as I have described above.

## 71

### QUINCE

In Tierra Firme there is a fruit that the Christians call quince,[74] but it is not a quince. But they are the same size, and round and yellow. The skin is green and bitter. The fruit is peeled and quartered, and the seeds which are bitter are removed. Then the fruit is placed in a pot and cooked with meat or other things, and it makes a very tasty and nourishing dish. The trees on which this fruit grows are not large, and look more like shrubs than trees. There are a great many of these, and the leaves are about the same as those of the quince in Spain.

## 72

### AVOCADO

In Tierra Firme there are trees called pear trees, but they are not the same as Spanish pear trees although they are in no way inferior. Rather, they have such fruit [avocado, *Persea gratissima*] that they are superior to the pears here. They are large trees with wide leaves resembling somewhat those of the laurel, but they are larger and greener. This tree bears pears that weigh about a pound, although there are some larger, some smaller. They have the same color and shape as true pears. The skin is thicker and they are softer. In the center there is a seed about the size of a large chestnut that has been husked, like that of the mammee. It is in one piece, however, while the mammee seed is in three; but it is bitter and of the same

---

74. This may be the plant called *membrillo de montaña*, 'mountain quince' (*Gustavia augusta*).

shape. On this seed there is a very thin membrane, and between it and the skin is the edible portion. There is a goodly amount of flesh that is very tasty and the juice and flesh taste much like butter. It is a good fruit of good flavor. These trees are well cared for and prized by those who have them. These trees, like all those I have described, are wild. The principal gardener is God, because the Indians give these trees no care whatsoever. These pears are very good with cheese. The fruit is gathered early, before it matures, and put aside. When they ripen, they develop a good flavor and are perfect to eat. Once they are ripe they must be eaten, because they spoil if they are left too long.

### 73
### CALABASH TREE

The calabash[75] tree is a medium-sized tree, sometimes large, according to where it grows. They bear round gourd-like fruit which are called *higueras,* from which the Indians make cup-like vessels for drinking. In some parts of Tierra Firme they make such graceful and handsome ones of such high polish that any prince would be pleased to drink from them. They attach gold handles to these vessels. They are very clean, and water tastes very good in them. These vessels are quite necessary and useful for drinking because the Indians of most of Tierra Firme do not have other vessels.

### 74
### JOBO TREE

The jobo trees [hog plums, *Spondias lutea*] are large, beautiful, graceful trees casting a very healthful shadow. There are a great many of them and the fruit is very tasty, of good odor and color. They are like small yellow plums, but the stone is very large, leaving only a small edible part. They are harmful to the teeth if eaten often, since they have sprigs attached to the stone which penetrate the gums when a man tries to separate them from the edible part of the fruit. When the shoots of this plant are boiled in water, it makes a fine dressing for the beard and to wash the legs, and it is of good odor. The

---

75. Alvarez López says there are two species, *Crescentia cujete* and *Crescentia cucurbitina* (p. 218).

bark of this tree, boiled in water, gives a liquid that, when rubbed on the legs, acts as an astringent and greatly relieves weariness. It makes a most excellent refreshing and salutary bath. This is the best tree in that land to sleep under, for it does not give one a headache as is the case with some other trees. Since in that land Christians are accustomed to roam the country, this has been proved. And as soon as they find hog plum trees they hang their hammocks or beds under them in order to sleep there.

## 75

## GUAYACAN

In the Indies as well as in Spain and other nations, the *palo santo,* called by the Indians *guayacán,* is famous.[76] I shall describe it briefly. The tree is somewhat smaller than the walnut. There are many forests of these trees in Hispaniola and on the other islands, but I have not seen any on Tierra Firme nor have I heard of anyone who has seen one there. The bark of this tree is spotted with green and brown like a blossom-colored or speckled horse.

The leaves are like those of the strawberry-tree[77] but somewhat smaller and greener. It bears small yellowish fruit, similar to two lupines, connected at the edges. It is very strong and hard wood, and has a heart almost black or dark gray. Since it is well known that the principal virtue of this wood is to cure syphilis, I shall not tarry long on my description except to say that splinters or filings of the wood are boiled in a certain quantity of water according to the amount of wood used. When the water has boiled down two parts or more, it is removed from the fire and allowed to settle. Those afflicted with the disease drink this potion early in the morning (for several days) on an empty stomach. They maintain a rigid diet. During the day they drink other water that has been boiled with guayacán. Undoubtedly many are cured of syphilis by this treatment.

But I am not describing in detail how this remedy is taken here, but how it is made in the Indies, where the wood is fresher. If anyone here needs this remedy, he should not treat

---

76. Alvarez López says (p. 218) that the *guayacán* is *Guaiacum officinale;* the *palo santo* is *Guaiacum sanctum.*
77. *Arbutus unedo.*

himself according to what I have written, for this is another land with more temperate and colder climate. Those sick of the disease here should take good care of themselves and use other measures. But still this remedy is widely used, and many in Spain know how to prepare it, and anyone who needs the treatment can learn how to prepare it from those who know. For those who need it, I recommend the best guayacán, which is found on the island of Beata.

Your Majesty may rest assured that this horrible disease came from the Indies. Although it is quite common among the natives, it is not so dangerous there as it is here in Europe. The Indians of the islands cure themselves very easily with this wood. In Tierra Firme they use in addition other herbs that they know, for they are expert herbalists.

Syphilis first appeared in Spain after Admiral Christopher Columbus discovered the Indies and returned home. Some Christians who accompanied Columbus on the voyage of discovery and some who were on the second voyage brought this plague to Spain. From them other people were contaminated. Later, in 1495, when the Great Captain, Gonzalo Fernández de Córdoba, went to Italy with an army to support young King Ferdinand of Naples against Charles VIII of France (he of the big head), directed there by the Catholic Sovereigns Ferdinand and Isabella of immortal memory, your Majesty's grandparents, the disease was carried to Italy for the first time by a few Spanish soldiers. Since that was the time when the French under King Charles were invading, the Italians called it the 'French disease,' and the French called it the 'Neapolitan disease' because they had not seen it before that war. From there it spread all over Christendom and was carried into Africa by men and women who had the disease. The disease is contracted most easily in sexual intercourse, as many persons have discovered. It can also be caught by eating from the same plates and drinking from the same glasses and cups used by those who have the disease, and especially by sleeping on the same sheets and bedclothes which they have used.

This disease is so serious and painful that no man can help seeing the many people, rotten and crippled like Saint Lazarus, who are afflicted with it. Likewise many people have died of it. Very few Christians who associate and lie with the Indian women have escaped the malady. But as I have said, in the

New World the disease is not so serious as it is here, because the tree that grows there is more beneficial, fresher, and more efficacious, and because the land is warm, and because the air and constellations are more propitious than here for those who suffer from this disease. Experience shows that the best trees for treating this malady are found on the island of Beata, which is near Santo Domingo of Hispaniola, off the south coast.

## 76

### GENIPAP

Among other trees of the islands and of Tierra Firme there is a tree called *jagua* [genipap, *Genipa americana*], and there are many of this species. They are tall, straight, and beautiful, and from them the Indians make good shafts for their lances, as long and as heavy as they desire them to be. They are of a beautiful texture and grayish white color. These trees bear fruit as large as the fruit of the opium poppy, which they resemble very much. The fruit is good to eat when it is ripe. From the fruit is obtained a clear liquid which the Indians use to bathe their legs, and at times even their whole bodies, when they feel that the flesh is soft and flabby. They even paint themselves with it for the mere pleasure. The liquid has a strong astringent effect, and gradually turns to a jet black any part of the flesh or nails that it touches. This stain will not disappear until twelve or fifteen days or more have passed, nor does it leave the nails, if once they have been blackened, until they grow out, or by cutting them gradually as they grow. I and others have tested this. Since in the New World there are many rivers to ford, the said genipap is very good to rub on the legs from the knees down.

Often the men play tricks on the women by surreptitiously sprinkling them with this liquid mixed with fragrant water. Then more moles appear on their skin than they desire. The woman who is ignorant of the cause of this is eager to look for cures all of which are harmful and more likely to burn or damage the face than remove the black spot. But after a time, little by little, as it runs its course, the spot will disappear.

When the Indians go into battle they paint themselves with this genipap and with annatto, which is a sort of red ochre, only the annatto is much redder. The Indian women are also fond of this paint.

### 77

### MANCHINEEL

The manchineel apples,[78] from which the Carib Indians make the poison with which they tip their arrows, are borne on very bushy trees with many thick limbs and branches and very green leaves similar to those of the pear tree, except that they are smaller and more round. The trees produce this evil fruit in great abundance. The fruit is like the perfectly round pears of Sicily or Naples, in shape like small early pears. In some places they are spotted red and have a very pleasant odor. These trees usually grow on the coast near the sea, and every man who sees them wants to eat many of the pears or manchineel apples. From these manchineel apples, from the large ants that cause the swellings described above, from vipers and other poisonous things, the Carib Indians make the deadly poison with which they tip their arrows and darts.

These manchineel trees grow, as I have said, near the water. All the Christians in that land who serve your Majesty believe that there is no antidote so efficacious for this poison as sea water. They wash the wound well, and in this way some have recovered, but not many. Even though sea water may be an antidote, and perhaps it is, they do not know exactly how to make use of the remedy. Out of every fifty Christians wounded by this poison, not three escape. So that your Majesty may better comprehend the power of the poison of this tree, I say that if a man lies down to sleep for only an hour in the shade of one of these manchineel trees, he awakes with his head and eyes swollen, his eyebrows level with his cheeks. If by chance a drop of dew falls from this tree into a man's eyes, his eyes will burst, or at least the man will go blind. It would be very difficult to describe the pestiferous properties of those trees. There are a great many of them ranging from the Gulf of Urabá on the north coast to the west coast, so many that they are numberless. When the wood of the tree is burned one cannot bear it, because instantly it gives one a splitting headache.

78. *Hippomane mancinella*.

## 78
## BIG TREES

There are such big trees[79] in Tierra Firme that I would not dare describe them if I did not have many to corroborate what I say.

About a league from Darién, or the city of Santa María del Antigua, there runs a wide and deep river called the Cutí. There the Indians have a big tree which crosses the whole river from bank to bank, over which they pass and over which persons once in that area but now living in this Court have passed many times. And I am one of them. This tree was very high and thick and had been there for some time, so it was gradually sinking in the middle, and for a small space one had to walk in water almost to the knees while crossing. Therefore, when I was your Majesty's Justice in that city three years ago, in 1522, I had another tree cut down, a little down stream from the one mentioned above, and it crossed the whole river with more than fifty feet to spare on the opposite bank. This tree also was thicker and lay more than three feet above the surface of the water. As it fell it knocked down other trees and branches of the trees on the opposite bank, and brought down some of the grape vines I have already described. They contained many big black grapes and the fifty of us who were there ate many of them. That tree was more than sixteen spans thick at the greatest diameter, but it was much smaller than many other trees in that land.

The Indians of the coast and province of Cartagena make *canoas* [dugouts] of these trees. A dugout is a boat in which they sail. Some of these dugouts are so large they will carry one hundred to one hundred and thirty men. The boat is of one piece, made from the trunk of one tree. Some are wide enough to hold a cask or barrel, with enough room on each side for the people to pass from one end of the dugout to the other. Some are ten to twelve spans wide. These boats are operated with two sails, a mainsail and a foresail, made of very good cotton.

The largest tree[80] which I have seen in that land, or in any

---

79. These must be the ceiba (*Ceiba pentandra*) or the *Copaifera hemitomophylla*.
80. Here Alvarez López and Miranda think Oviedo definitely means the Ceiba tree (*Casearia pentandra* or *Ceiba pentandra*).

other, was in the province of Guaturo in 1522. Since the chief of that province was in rebellion against your Majesty, I went in search of him and arrested him. On the way my men and I passed over a range of mountains covered with big trees. On the top of the mountain we found a tree, among others, with three roots or parts in the form of a triangle, something like a tripod, and the opening from root to root was more than twenty feet, and it was so high that a side cart with stakes, the sort of cart on which stakes are placed here in the Kingdom of Toledo at the time grain is harvested, could easily pass through any one of the three openings. At a height more than a lance length from the ground the three tremendous trunks or feet came together and formed a single tree or trunk. The lowest limbs of the tree were higher than the tower of San Román of the city of Toledo. From that point on to the top of the tree, there were many large branches. Some Spaniards climbed the tree, and I was among them, and from the point I reached, which was near the place branches began to grow, one could get a marvelous view of the land as it stretched away towards the province of Abrayme. The tree was covered with vines, and these were very safe ladders to climb. Each 'foot' of this tree that I have described was more than twenty spans thick, and where they joined in one trunk the tree was more than forty-five spans in circumference. I named that mountain the peak of the Tripod Tree. All this was seen by the people who were with me at that time in the year 1522, when I captured the above-mentioned chief of the province of Guaturo.

There are many good varieties of wood there, fragrant cedars, black palms, and mangrove trees, and many other species, some being so heavy they will not float in water but sink to the bottom. Others are as light as cork. But in reality all these things could not possibly be described in the few pages of this narrative or summary.

Since we are now dealing with trees, and before proceeding to another subject, I want to explain how the Indians build fires with sticks. They take a stick about two spans long and as thick as the little finger, or the size of an arrow, that is slick and smooth, of a very hard wood they use for this purpose. And when they stop to kindle a fire, they select two of the lightest and driest sticks they can find and place them very close together, like two fingers held tight together,

## ¶Aruoles grandes.  Cap.lxxviij.

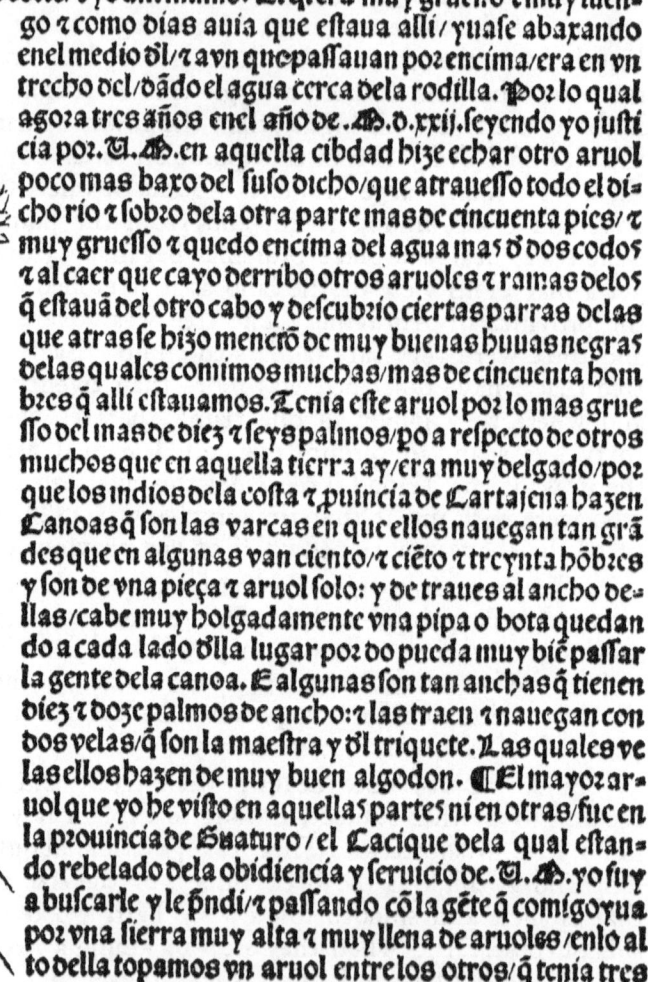

En tierra firme ay tan grandes aruoles que si yo hablasse en parte que no ouiesse tantos testigos de vista/con temor lo osaria dezir. Digo que a vna legua del Darien o cibdad de sca Maria del antigua passa vn rio harto ancho y muy hondo que se llama el Cuti y los Indios teniã vn aruol gruesso atrauessado de parte a parte/ que tomaua todo el dicho rio/ por el qual passaron muchas vezes algunos que en aquellas partes hã estado que agora estan en esta corte/ y yo assi mismo. El ql era muy gruesso y muy luengo y como dias auia que estaua alli/ yua se abaxando enel medio dl/ y avn que passauan por encima/era en vn trecho del/ dãdo el agua cerca de la rodilla. Por lo qual agora tres años enel año de. M.d.xxij. seyendo yo justicia por. V.M. en aquella cibdad hize echar otro aruol poco mas baxo del suso dicho/ que atrauesso todo el dicho rio y sobro dela otra parte mas de cincuenta pies/ y muy gruesso y quedo encima del agua mas d dos codos y al caer que cayo derribo otros aruoles y ramas delos q estauã del otro cabo y descubrio ciertas parras delas que atras se hizo mencio de muy buenas huuas negras delas quales comimos muchas/ mas de cincuenta hombres q alli estauamos. Tenia este aruol por lo mas gruesso del mas de diez y seys palmos/ pe a respecto de otros muchos que en aquella tierra ay/ era muy delgado/ por que los indios dela costa y puincia de Cartajena hazen Canoas q son las varcas en que ellos nauegan tan grãdes que en algunas van ciento/ y ciẽto y treynta hõbres y son de vna pieça y aruol solo: y de traues al ancho dellas/ cabe muy holgadamente vna pipa o bota quedando a cada lado d lla lugar por do pueda muy biẽ passar la gente dela canoa. E algunas son tan anchas q tienen diez y doze palmos de ancho: y las traen y nauegan con dos velas/ q son la maestra y dl triquete. Las quales velas ellos hazen de muy buen algodon. ¶El mayor aruol que yo he visto en aquellas partes ni en otras/ fue en la prouincia de Suaturo/ el Cacique dela qual estando rebelado dela obidiencia y seruicio de. V.M. yo fuy a buscarle y le pndi/ y passando cõ la gẽte q comigo yua por vna sierra muy alta y muy llena de aruoles/ en lo al to della topamos vn aruol entre los otros/ q tenia tres

and between the two they place the point of their 'fire' stick, which they twist rapidly between their palms by rubbing the palms back and forth. As the point of the stick wears into the other sticks on the ground, they catch fire in a very short time, and this is the way they build a fire.

I should also like to tell what I remember about certain logs in that land, which may also be found on occasion in Spain. They are decayed trunks of trees that have fallen a long time ago, and are very light and white and at night shine like live coals. When the Spanairds find these logs, and go to make war on some province at night, sometimes it is necessary to travel over territory where no one knows the way. The first Christian who follows the Indian guide takes a stick from one of these fallen trees and places it in his cap, back over his shoulders, and the second man can follow him closely and safely by following the glowing piece of wood. The second man also carries a piece of this wood, and behind him the third does likewise, and so on. They all carry glowing sticks and so no one loses the way followed by the leaders. Since this light can not be seen very far away it is a very good guide, since the Spaniards can not be discovered or seen from a distance.

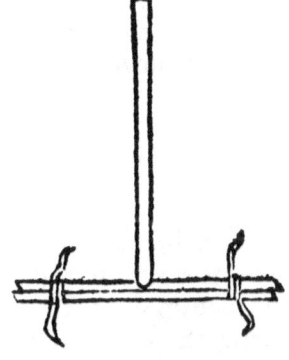

*Making Fire with Sticks*

I remember that Pliny in his *Natural History* expressly mentions trees that remain green and never lose their leaves, such as the laurel, citron, orange, olive, and others. In all he cites about five or six. In this regard I say that in the islands and Tierra Firme it would be difficult to find two trees that lose their leaves at any time. Although I have looked for it, I have not found any tree that loses its leaves, not even the orange, lemon, palm, pomegranate, and citron nor any others which were carried there from Spain, except the cassia fistula. This last tree does lose its leaves and also has another peculiarity. Other trees and plants in the Indies send their roots down only about seven feet below the surface of the soil more or less, because of the heat or contrary conditions that would be found at the lower depth, while the drumstick

95

tree sends its roots down until they touch water. No other plant or tree in the Indies does that.

May what I have said suffice regarding trees, because it really is the matter for a long history, which I do not have time for now.

## 79

## CANE

In the chapter above I did not want to include a description of cane, nor do I want to include this in the chapter on plants since they deserve a separate section. In Tierra Firme there are many different species of cane and in many places houses are built of them and covered with the shoots. Even the walls are made of cane as I have described. There are some very large canes as big as a man's thigh, one joint, or internode, being more than three spans long and containing more than one large jugful, or four gallons, of water. There are other smaller ones that make excellent quivers for arrows.

In Tierra Firme there is one remarkable species of cane, about the size of a lance shaft, with each internode being more than two spans long. They grow far away from each other. Usually they are found about twenty-two to thirty paces apart or even more. Others will not be found for two or three leagues. They do not grow in all provinces, and always they are found very near very tall trees; they grow close to the tree and go into the tree's branches, then turn back to the ground. The sections of these canes are all filled with excellent clear water which does not taste of the cane or any other thing. It is as good as if it were taken from the best spring in the world, and it has never harmed anyone who drank it. Often Christians traveling through that land, in dry areas and wanting water and about to die of thirst, have come upon these canes, and not one has suffered ill effects from drinking of them regardless of how much he has drunk. When they find the cane they cut them in sections, each man carrying two or three internodes, or as many as he can, so for the rest of the journey he can carry one or two half-gallons of water. Even if it is carried for several days over a long journey, the water remains fresh.

## 80
## PLANTS AND HERBS

Since I have recorded all that my poor memory retains concerning trees in the New World, I want to pass on to a description of the plants and herbs of that land. I will dismiss with a few words those in Tierra Firme that resemble some in Spain in appearance or taste or in any detail. Trees, plants, and herbs which have been carried from Spain to Hispaniola and the other islands that have been conquered, and which have already been described, are to be found in Tierra Firme too. These include sweet and sour oranges, lemons, citrons, vegetables, and good melons that bear all the year. There is also a native sweet basil found in many places, and also native nightshade and purslane. These last three are native to the New World and are in appearance, size, taste, odor, and fruit like those in Castile.

In addition to these, there is much wild cress, which in taste is precisely like that here in Spain. However, the stems are thicker and the leaves larger. Likewise there is very good coriander, like ours in taste. However, the leaf is different; it is wide and has very annoying small spines in it. However it can be eaten. Also there is clover, of the same fragrance as ours in Spain, but with many leaves and a handsome stem bearing a white flower. The leaves are long and as large or larger than those of the laurel.

There is another herb almost like the lesser bindweed except that its stems are smaller, and the leaves usually somewhat broader. It is called 'Y.'[81] It grows in great abundance, and swine are very fond of it and grow fat on it. The Christians use it as a purgative. This excellent purgative can be given to a child or a pregnant woman without ill effects, for the person who takes it will have no more than three or four bowel movements. The herb is well mashed and the juice is strained, and in order that it may lose some of its rawness, a small amount of sugar is added, and a very small bowl of it is taken on an empty stomach. This potion is not bitter, and can be drunk without adding either sugar or honey. Not always do the Christians have the sugar to put in this juice. Most of those who take this medicine benefit from it and praise it.

81. This is the *Ipomoea bona-nox*.

In the matter of purgatives, I happen to remember 'hazelnuts'[82] with which one should be very careful. I have seen some persons who were not benefited or purged at all by them, whereas other persons were so damaged in the stomach that they became seriously ill or even died. Because of the violence of this medication, one must exercise care and discretion in taking it. These 'hazelnut' trees grow in Hispaniola and the other islands. I have not seen them nor do I have evidence that they are found in Tierra Firme. They are plants almost as large as trees, and bear clusters of reddish catkins or umbels produced at the end of the stem like the seeds of fennel, and in those are produced the hazelnuts, which they resemble and taste like, and even better. In Spain they are well known and many people like them.

There are other plants called *ajes* [yams][83] and others called *batatas* [sweet potatoes, *Ipomoea batatas*]. They are planted from slips, and the stems and the leaves look like those of the lesser bindweed[84] or ivy running along the ground. But the leaves are not as large as ivy leaves. Beneath the surface of the earth they produce roots somewhat like turnips or carrots. The yams are purplish blue in color, and the sweet potatoes are somewhat tan. Roasted they are excellent eating, but the sweet potatoes are better.

Likewise there are melons[85] that the Indians plant. They grow as big as a half or a whole peck measure. Some are so large that an Indian has difficulty carrying one on his back. The flesh is white, in some yellow, and the seeds are almost like those of squash. This is a highly prized food, and is much better than squash, which it resembles. These melons will keep a long time and are highly regarded by the Indians.

There are many squash and eggplants grown from seeds carried there from Spain. The eggplants thrive in this new land, just as the Negro does in Guinea. An eggplant often grows five or six feet high or even taller. Usually the stalk of the plant is a little more than waist high. They produce fruit the whole year on the same plant, just as orange trees and fig trees do in that land.

82. *Jatropha multifida*.
83. Alvarez López says (p. 220) that the yam is in the *Convolvulaceae* family and not *Dioscoreaceae*, as described by Humboldt and repeated by many others.
84. *Convolvulus arvensis*.
85. These large melons could be *Cucurbita pepo* or *Cucumis anguria* (Alvarez López, p. 221).

There is one fruit that they call *piñas* [pineapple, *Ananas sativus*] that is produced on plants like thistles in the manner of aloes with many pulpy leaves, but more slender than those of the aloe, and longer and spiny. In the middle of the plant rises a stalk about three feet high and about two fingers thick, and on that a thick pineapple somewhat smaller than a child's head. Ordinarily they are somewhat smaller, and covered with scales, some higher than others, just as they are on pine cones. These scales do not separate and break, but form a sort of bark about the thickness of the rind of a melon. And when they are yellow, that is about a year after the plant has been placed in the ground, they are ripe enough to be eaten. Some mature in less time. And sometimes on the stem of the pineapple there are one or two shoots, and one on the top of the fruit. This shoot is planted in the soil and it takes root, and within a year produces another pineapple. The stalk on which the pineapple is borne, after the pineapple is plucked, is useless and will not bear fruit thereafter.

When the Indians and Christians plant pineapples, they put them in regular rows like vine stalks in a vineyard. This fruit smells better than peaches, and the whole house will be filled with this fragrance by one or two pineapples. In taste it is one of the best fruits in the world; it is also very handsome. In taste it is somewhat like peaches. The pineapple flesh is also much like that of a peach, but it has very fine filaments like the thistle, which are harmful to the teeth if one regularly eats this fruit. The pineapple is very juicy, and in some places the Indians make some good wine of it. It is a healthful fruit and is given to sick people. For those who are surfeited and do not wish to eat, it is an excellent appetizer.

There are some trees [cacti] in the Island Hispaniola that are very spiny,[86] and I have never seen any plant or tree that is so wild or ugly. I have not been able to determine whether they are trees or shrubs. They have branches covered with pulpy leaves that are wide, shapeless, and ugly. The branches are originally leaves, and as they grow longer and harder, other pulpy leaves grow from them. It would be very difficult to describe this plant with words; it would be much more satisfactory to make a sketch of it for through the eyes one might understand what cannot be described with words. The

---

86. *Opuntia triacantha*.

plant is good for one thing. The flesh and leaves are pounded to a pulp and spread on a piece of cloth. This is used to bind up a broken arm or leg. Even if the limb has been broken in many places, it knits and heals completely within a fortnight. Until this poultice has produced a cure, it holds so tight to the flesh that it is difficult to remove. But as soon as the bone has knit, the poultice comes off without assistance. There are many people there who can vouch for the efficacy of this treatment.

There are other plants that the Christians call *plátanos* [banana trees, *Musa sapientum*]. These are tall plants, like trees, with a trunk as large as a man's thigh. From bottom to top grow tremendous leaves, ten or twelve palms long and more than three wide. These leaves are broken off by the wind and their heavy stems remain. At the top of the stalk there grows a bunch of forty or fifty bananas, and each banana is a palm and a half long and as large as a man's wrist, more or less. Naturally the size depends upon the fertility of the soil, and in some places they are much smaller. They do not have a very thick skin, which is very easy to remove. Inside it is all flesh which is very much like the marrow of the legbone of a cow. The whole bunch is cut, then it turns yellow and is hung in the house where the bananas ripen. This is very good fruit; and when the fruit is peeled and dried in the sun, like figs, it is very good and pleasant fruit, being much better than dried figs. When roasted in the oven on a tile, it is very good, being like a sweet tasty conserve.

These bananas are picked green and carried to sea, and last some days. They ripen in about two weeks and are better at sea than on land. They are not really improved by the voyage, but at sea many things commonly had on land are not available and so any fruit there is tasty and highly prized.

It requires a year for this trunk—stalk would be more accurate—to produce fruit, and during that time there grow up around it ten or twelve slips or offspring exactly like the parent plant. These in turn will produce fruit and other plants, just as the parent plants have done. As soon as the bunch of fruit is cut, the plant begins to dry, and then it is cut down whenever the natives choose, because it only occupies valuable space. There are so many of these plants and they multiply so rapidly that it is difficult to believe

## Plantas y yeruas.

nos: y es carnosa como el durazno saluo que tiene briznas como el cardo, pero muy sotiles: mas es dañosa quando se continua a comer para los dientes: y es muy çumosa, y en algunas partes los indios hazen vino dellas, y es bueno, τ son tan sanas q̃ se dan a dolientes, τ les abre mucho el apetite a los q̃ tienẽ hastio τ perdida la gana del comer. ⁋Unos aruoles ay en la ysla española espinosos: q̃ al parescer ningun aruol ni planta se podria ver de mas saluajez, ni tan feo, τ segũ la manera dellos yo no me sabria determinar ni dezir si son aruoles, o plantas, hazẽ vnas ramas llenas de vnas pencas anchas τ disformes o de muy mal parescer: las quales ramas primero fue cada vna vna penca, como las otras y de aq̃llas endurescien̄dose τ alongãdose salẽ las otras pencas: finalmẽte es de manera q̃ es dificultoso de escriuir su forma: τ para darse a entẽder seria necessario pintarse paraque por medio de la vista se cõprehendiesse lo que la lengua falta en esta parte. para lo q̃ es bueno este aruol o planta es que majando las dichas pencas mucho y tẽdido aq̃llo a manera de emplasto en vn paño, τ ligado vna pierna o braço con ello avn q̃ este q̃brada en muchos pedaços en espacio de quinze dias lo suelda, τ junta como si nunca se quebrara, τ hasta q̃ aya hecho su operacion esta tan aferrada τ asida esta medecina con la carne, que es muy dificultosa de la despegar: pero assi como ha curado el mal y hecho su operacion, luego ella por si misma se aparta y despega de aquel lugar donde la auian puesto: y deste efecto y remedio q̃ es dicho ay mucha espiriencia por los muchos q̃ lo han prouado. ⁋Ay assi mismo vnas plantas q̃ los xp̃ianos llamã platanos, los quales son altos como aruoles y se hazen gruessos en el tronco como vn gruesso muslo de vn hombre, o algo mas, y desde abaxo arriba echa vnas hojas longuissimas τ muy anchas τ tãto que tres palmos o mas son anchas, y mas de diez o doze palmos de longura, las q̃les hojas despues el ayre rompe quedãdo entero el lomo dellas. En el medio de ste cogollo en lo alto nasce vn razimo con quarenta o cinquenta platanos y mas y menos: y cada platano es tan luengo como palmo y medio, y de la grosseza de la muñeca de vn braço, poco mas o menos, segun la fertilidad de la tierra donde nascen: porq̃ en algunas partes son muy menores: tienen vna corteza no muy gruessa τ facil de rõper y de dẽtro todo es medula: que dessollado o quitada la dicha corteza paresce vn tuetano de vna caña de vaca

*Leaf of a Banana Tree*

without seeing it. They are very succulent, and often when they are pulled up by the roots, a great quantity of water runs out. And in the hole where they grew it seems that all the humidity of the soil and the water beneath have been drawn to that place and to the stalk.

Ants are very fond of these bananas and are to be found in great numbers on the stalk and branches. In some places there have been so many ants that the plants have been pulled up and thrown away outside the towns, for the plant could not thrive because of the great number of ants.

There are bananas throughout the year. They are not, however, native to those parts, because the first bananas were carried there from Spain. However, they have multiplied so greatly that it is marvelous to see the great abundance of them on the islands and in Tierra Firme, where the Christians have settled. And they are larger, better, and more tasty than those in Spain.

There are some wild plants which grow in the fields. I have seen them only on the Island of Hispaniola, although they grow on other islands and in other parts of the Indies. They are called *tunas* [prickly pear, *Opuntia spp.*] and grow from very spiny thistle-like plants, and bear fruit also called *tunas*. The fruit resembles large figs, and has little crowns like those of the medlar. Inside they are very red, and have small seeds and a skin like figs. They are very tasty and the fields are covered with them. After one eats three or four of them (or better, more) if the one who has eaten them stops to urinate, the urine is as red as real blood. This happened to me the first time I ate of them. After an hour I wanted to urinate (this fruit is very conducive to such), and when I saw the color of the urine, I was in grave fear as to the condition of my health. I was sorely afraid that some serious malady had come upon me. Indeed my imagination could have caused me much grief if persons of more experience and of longer time in that area had not informed me of the cause.

There are some plants called *bijaos* [wild plantain, *Heliconia bihai*], which have straight twigs and very wide leaves that the Indians often use in making very good covers for their houses. Sometimes when it rains the natives place the leaves over their heads to protect themselves from the water. They also make baskets which they call *jabas*, in which they place clothes or other things. These baskets are well woven, and in them the wild plantain is interwoven. They are thoroughly waterproof, and even if it rains much on them or if they are placed in a river, the contents never get wet. These baskets are made from the bark of the shoots of the wild plantain. They also make baskets to hold salt and other things. They are all well made and graceful. Besides, when the Indians are in the country and find themselves short on provisions, they pull up the young wild plantain and eat the root or the part that is under the soil. It is tender and not of bad taste, resembling young tender rush roots.

Since I have come to the end of my narrative regarding these things, I want to say one thing that has some connection. The Indians use bark and leaves to dye and color their cotton cloth. They color it black, tan, green, blue, yellow, and red, the colors being as vivid or as subdued as the Indians desire. The colors could not be more perfect. After boiling the bark and leaves in a pot, without changing the dye, they can produce all the distinct colors noted above. I think this difference is due to the quality, characteristics, and capacity for taking color of the things they put into the dye, such as yarn, cloth, or other things they want to give the above colors or any one of them.

81

## OTHER THINGS OF INTEREST

I might describe many other things, but since I find my memory hazy, I shall omit those I am not completely sure of. However, I do want to describe some insects that are a fearful pest to man. These insects make man realize that even worthless and petty things can disturb his peace of mind, and that he should not forget the chief end of man, which is to know his Creator and seek the salvation of his soul. The way is open and clear to Christians and to all those who will open their eyes to understanding.

Although some of the things I am about to describe are filthy and not as clean and as agreeable as those already described, nevertheless they are worthy of being noted, so one can see the many things in nature.

In many parts of Tierra Firme the Indians and the Christians wear loose trousers rolled up, because there is much water, and when they cross the fields many ticks on the bushes stick to them. They are small as grains of finely-ground salt, and they cause the legs to thicken and swell. There is only one way they can be removed from the flesh, and that is by covering the legs or other infested parts with oil. Then the insects can be scraped away with a knife. The Indians who do not have oil, burn them out and suffer intense pain in the operation.

Only rarely are Christians in the new world bothered by the small pestiferous insects that grow in a man's hair and on his body. Because after we pass the line of the diameter where the compass needle changes from northeast to northwest, which is only a short distance beyond the Azores as we continue the voyage to the West, all the lice on the men's heads and bodies die, and as I have said, the Spaniards are clean and little by little all vermin disappear and are not to be seen. No Christian in the Indies, except a few children born there, have vermin on their bodies. Most Indians, however, do have them in their hair. This is especially true in the province of Cueba, which extends for more than a hundred leagues and touches both the North and South Coast. The Indians delouse each other. The women are the best flea cleaners. They eat all the vermin they can catch, and it is with difficulty that we can prevent our own household servants from doing so, since they come from the province of Cueba.

In all this one interesting thing can be observed. Even though we do not have these vermin in our hair and on our bodies while we are in the Indies, when we are returning to Europe, as we reach the place in the Atlantic where the vermin left us on the westward trip, once again we are attacked, as if the lice were lying in wait for us. And it requires several days to rid oneself of them, even if a man changes his shirt two or three times a day. The lice are so small that they are almost as small as nits. Soon we are able to free ourselves of them, however, and only men who are lax in matters of personal cleanliness are bothered. I have seen all this happen several times, since I have crossed the Atlantic four times following this course.

In many places the Indians are sodomites. The Indian chiefs and lords publicly have boys with whom they commit this damnable sin. As soon as these boys begin this practice they put on the short cotton skirt of the Indian women, which extends from the waist to the knees. They also wear bead bracelets and necklaces and other adornments usually worn by women. These boys do not go to war nor do they occupy themselves with other labors of men. Rather they work in the house, sweeping, cleaning, and on other customary duties of the women. These boys are hated most violently by the women. The women, however, are very submissive to their husbands and do not dare speak of this often except to the Christians. These boys are called in the Cueba language *camayoa*. And when one Indian wants to insult another or say he is effeminate, he calls him *camayoa*.

According to what they themselves say, the Indians in some provinces exchange wives. The one who gets the older woman considers himself the winner in the bargain because the older women are more readily inclined to hard work.

The Indians are very expert in extracting salt from seawater. Those who make salt on the dike of Zeeland near the town of Middleburg get no better results. The salt produced by the Indians is just as white or whiter, and is much stronger, and it does not lose its savor so quickly. I have seen salt from both places and have seen it made in both places.

Many people are of the opinion that there are precious stones in the Indies. I do not refer to New Spain, because precious stones have been brought from there to Spain, and in Valladolid last year, 1524, while your Majesty was there, I saw an emerald that had been brought from Yucatan or New Spain. On it was carved in relief a round face, in the fashion of a dark green agate, which sold for more than four hundred ducats of good gold. But in Santa Marta, of Tierra Firme, when the armada sent by the Catholic Sovereign Ferdinand to Castilla de Oro touched there, I went ashore with others and we got a thousand odd *pesos* of gold and certain pieces of cloth and other things that belonged to the Indians on which were emeralds, cornelians, jasper, chalcedony, white sapphires, and amber. All these things were found there and it is believed that these things have come from inland through trade and commerce that those Indians carried on with other tribes. The Indians more than any people in the world are inclined to barter, sell, and trade things. Their dugouts go from one place to another, and they carry salt where it is needed, and in exchange they receive gold or cloth or cotton thread, slaves, fish, or other things.

Sinú is a province of arrow-shooting Carib Indians, which borders upon the province of Cartagena and lies between the latter province and Caribana Point. Once Pedrarias de Avila, Governor of Castilla del Oro for your Majesty, sent certain people there and they were routed, and Captain Diego de Bustamante and other Spaniards were killed. This party found many baskets the size of those that come filled with sea breams from the mountain of Biscay. They were filled with cicadas, locusts, and crickets. The Indians said they were prisoners forced to carry those baskets to other places inland, far from the coast, where they do not have fish and where the natives are very fond of that food. They said that they received in payment things which they needed and liked, and things that those people had in abundance, and that in this case they were paid in cicadas and crickets.

## 82

## GOLD MINES

I can speak of the interesting subject of gold mines more fully than any other person. For twelve years I have been overseer of the mining and smelting of gold for his Catholic Majesty Ferdinand, God rest his soul, and now for your Majesty. In this capacity I have had the opportunity to see how the gold is mined, and I know well how rich that land is. I have also had my Indians and slaves mine gold for me.

I can affirm as an eyewitness that all over Castilla del Oro, which is in Tierra Firme, there are many rich gold mines, and that no one could ask me to find a gold mine but that I could locate one within ten leagues, and it certainly has been worth my while to search for them. Gold is found everywhere, but naturally in some places it is more plentiful than in others. In working a vein or mine one must keep in mind the location, cost, people available, and other things necessary in obtaining the metal so that one can make a profit, for there is no doubt that gold can be found in most places. The gold that is found in Castilla del Oro is very good, running from twenty-two carats or above. In addition to the large quantity of gold extracted from the mines, there are vast treasures of wrought gold in the possession of the Indians who have already been conquered. They give this to the Spaniards willingly as friends or for their own ransom, and some of it is very good. Most of the wrought gold possessed by the Indians is base, containing copper. They make it into jewels and ornaments with which the men and women adorn their bodies. In fact, it is the thing which they esteem and prize above all others.

Gold is found either in streams or stream beds or on the *sabana* [savanna], the name given to plains, meadows, and hills that are treeless, and to all cleared land, whether it is covered with grass or not. Occasionally gold is found some distance inland, away from the rivers where there are trees, and in order to dig it out many large trees must be felled.

I should like to describe the two methods employed in obtaining gold, the one in streams and ravines and the other in the level ground. If the lode or vein is located on a savanna or clear place, the Indians clean away everything on the surface of the ground over a square of eight or ten feet; then they dig down a distance of one or two spans. Then without digging deeper they wash all the loose dirt of that area. If they find gold within that area they follow the vein, if not they dig down the same distance and wash the dirt as before. This they continue until gradually, washing all the dirt, they strike solid rock. If they have not discovered gold before reaching the rock, they discontinue mining in that area and move to a new place. But if they do find gold, they continue working at the level they discover it until the vein is exhausted, if they believe the reward will merit such. The length and width of the excavation naturally is determined by the extent of the deposit. Only the discoverer can remove gold from that mine, but adjoining it anyone can stake out a claim for himself.

These mines on the savannas should be sought for near rivers, streams, or ravines, or some water supply so that the gold may be more easily worked. There Indians are put to digging and clearing the earth from the mines, then they fill trays with the earth, which other Indians carry to the streams for panning. Those who carry the trays do not wash the earth, but pour the earth in other trays for the washers (for the most part Indian women, because the work is easier) and then return for another load.

The washers sit on the bank with their feet up to their knees in the water. They hold the tray by the two handles or ends, they dip up a little water, skillfully pouring it out again, and there enters the tray only the amount of water the Indian wants. Gradually the earth is poured out with the water, and if there is any gold it settles to the bottom of the tray. These trays are concave and about the same size as a barber's basin and almost as deep. After all the earth has been washed out, the gold remains in the bottom of the tray. That gold is placed aside and the tray is refilled to repeat the operation.

And thus in this fashion each washer continues and gets out in one day as much gold as God wills, and according to the luck that the overseer of the Indians and other people who are occupied in this work may have. It should be noted that for each two Indians that wash the earth, two Indians are needed to carry the earth to each of them, and two others who scrape the earth away and break and dig and fill service trays. For the trays in which the earth is carried to the washers are called service trays. And in addition, other people are needed in the houses where the Indians live and where they go to sleep at night. These people make bread and prepare the other food on which they are all sustained. So that for each tray usually, as has been said, at least five persons are employed.

The second manner of working or mining gold in a stream is as follows. The current of a stream is diverted from its bed and after the bed is dry and water has been bailed out (for 'to bail out' means to exhaust the water in the language of miners) gold may be found between the rocks and in the hollows and cracks of the rocks and in the part that was the main channel or natural bed of the stream. At times when one of the stream beds is good and rich a large quantity of gold is found in it. For your Majesty must remember the maxim, and it certainly appears to be true, that all gold originates in the hills and tops of the mountains and that the rains gradually wash it out and carry it down the rivers and other streams that rise in the mountains. However, gold is often found on plains, far removed from mountains. When this happens usually large quantities are found in that area. For the most part, however, gold is found on the slope of hills and in the bed of rivers and streams.

And so gold is usually mined in one of these two ways described above.

Since gold originates in the highlands and is washed down to the lowlands, one can deduce a very interesting fact. Coal never disintegrates beneath the surface when it comes from hard wood. And often when digging a mine on the slope or middle of a hill, or opening a mine in virgin soil, at a depth of from two to six yards or more coal is found at the same level as gold, and often before reaching gold. But in land that is thought to be virgin soil, and really is, in order to break and dig out coal that is there, one must remember that coal naturally could not have been deposited there except at the time when the surface of the earth was on the same level as the coal found there. The trees that originally stood in that place were torn down by the water and remained there. Then later it rained countless times and the waters brought down more and more soil from the higher levels until in the passing of countless years a great deposit of earth accumulated on the coal. So that gold mines are worked from the surface of the soil down to the depth that coal is found.

I say in addition that the further gold has been carried from the place of its origin to the place where it is discovered, the smoother and more purified it is, and of higher carat. The nearer it is found to the place of its origin, the rougher, less pure, and of lower carat it is. A large part of this gold turns out to be almost valueless when it is smelted. Often large nuggets are found, both above and below the surface of the earth.

The largest nugget that has been discovered in the Indies was the one lost in the sea near the island of Beata. It weighed three thousand two hundred *castellanos,* which is equal to one *arroba* and seven *libras,* or thirty-two *libras* of sixteen ounces,[87] which is equal to sixty-four gold marks. Many other nuggets have been found, but none so heavy as this one.

In 1515 I saw in the possession of your Majesty's treasurer, Miguel de Pasamonte, two nuggets. One weighed seven *libras,*

---

87. It has been estimated that this nugget weighed between fourteen and a half and fifteen kilograms (Alvarez López, p. 221).

which is fourteen *marcos,* and the other ten *marcos* or five *libras.* They were very good gold of at least twenty-two carats.

Since I am talking of gold it seems to me that before I go on to discuss some other subject, I should remark on the way the Indians are able to gild copper or base gold. They are able to give these metals such an excellent bright color that the metal they gild appears to be gold of at least twenty-two carats. They produce this color with certain herbs, and the most expert silversmiths of Spain or Italy, or wherever even better experts can be found, would be very happy and very rich if they had this secret or manner of gilding.

We have spoken in detail of the mines and also how the gold is removed from the soil. As for copper, I should like to say that large quantities of fine grade copper have been found in many parts of the islands and the mainland of the Indies, and each day more is found. But the people have not cared about it up to now and do not mine it. In other places this copper would be regarded as a great and useful treasure. But since there is so much gold, the richer removes importance from the poorer, and men do not mine the inferior metal.

In New Spain much very fine silver has been discovered, but as I said at the beginning of this narrative, I shall not describe anything in that province at present since it is all described in detail in my *General History of the Indies.*

## 83
## FISHES AND FISHING

In Tierra Firme I have seen a great abundance and many different species of fishes. Since it will be impossible to describe all of them here, I shall speak of a few. First I will say that there are broad sardines which have red tails; they are excellent food and among the best fish found there. There are also mojarras,[88] 'biajacas,'[89] jurels,[90] 'dajaos,'[91] rays and trout. These, and many others whose names I do not remember, are caught in great abundance in the rivers. Also very good shrimp are to be had there. Likewise some of the

---

88. *Eugerres plumieri.*    89. *Serranus inermis* or *Chromis fuscomaculatus.*
90. *Caranx latus.*    91. *Agonostomus monticola.*

above-named fish are caught in the sea, as well as pompanos,[92] acedias,[93] porgies, mullet, octopi, dolphins, very large shad, lobsters, crabs, oysters, and very large turtles. Very large sharks, manatees and morays are also caught there. There are many other fish and so many species and such a large quantity of them that it would require great space and time to describe them.

However, here I want to speak in detail only about three of these fish named above: the turtle, the shark, and the manatee. Beginning with the first, I say that in the island of Cuba large turtles[94] are found, sometimes so large that ten or fifteen men are necessary to pull one of them from the water. I have heard this from so many reliable people on that island that I consider it to be true. I can testify as an eyewitness about those killed in Tierra Firme. In the village of Acla I saw one so large that six men were hard put to it to carry it, and ordinarily the smaller ones are quite a burden for two men. The large one that I saw there carried by six men had a shell seven spans long, measured down the middle of its back, and more than five spans wide. The turtles are captured in the following manner: Often turtles are caught in drag nets, but the way in which they are caught in quantity is when they leave the sea to come out on the beach to lay their eggs or to feed. When the Spaniards or Indians find their tracks in the sand, they follow them. The turtles, being surprised, run toward the water, but since they are heavy and slow they are easily overtaken. Then a stick is placed under its front legs and as it runs along, the turtle is turned over on its back. Since the turtle cannot turn over from its back to an upright attitude, it must stay there. Leaving the turtle upside down, the hunters can follow tracks of any others that may be there, and handle that turtle in the same fashion. In this way many are caught. This is a very good fish of good flavor and healthful.

The second of the three fishes mentioned above is called *tiburón* [shark]. This fish is very large, swift in the water, and very bloodthirsty. Many are caught, especially the small ones, by the ships sailing the Atlantic or while at anchor and in other ways. The large ones are caught while the ships are

---

92. *Trachinotus galucus* and *T. ovatus*.   93. Flatfish, *Symphurus plagusia*.
94. *Chelone mydas*.

under way and in the following manner: when the shark sees a ship, it swims after the ship, eating the refuse and garbage thrown overboard. The shark can keep up with the ship regardless of its speed and even swim around it, and often follows the ship one hundred and fifty leagues or more. When the sailors want to catch one, they throw over the stern a hook about as thick as a thumb and about three palms long, bent in the fashion of other fishhooks and with its barb in proportion to its size; attached to the end of the shank of the hook are four or five heavy links of a chain, and in the last link is tied a line two or three times as big as the hook. On the hook they place a piece of fish or bacon or any kind of meat, or part of the entrails of another shark if they have killed one. In one day I have seen nine caught, and more could have been taken if they had been desired.

The shark follows the ship regardless of its speed, as I have said, and swallows the whole fishhook. As soon as the shark swallows the bait it tries to get away, but from the very force of the strike and from the tug of the ship the fishhook pierces the fish, and the point comes through its jaw, and the fish is caught. Some of these fish are so large that twelve to fifteen men or more are necessary to hoist and pull them on board. When they are in the boat a sailor kills the shark with several blows on the head from the flat side of an axe. Some of these fish are ten or twelve feet long or longer, and the widest are five, six, or seven spans wide. They have very big mouths in proportion to the body and have two separate rows of large fierce teeth, each row being quite distinct from the other. These fish are cut into strips and the strips hung in the open air on the rigging for two or three days. Then they can be eaten. The fish has a fine flavor, and because of its size furnishes food for the crew for several days. The young ones naturally are best and more tender and more easily digested. These fish are covered with skin, like the dogfish and spotted dogfish. For these fish as well as sharks are all viviparous. I mention this because Pliny in his *Natural History* does not include any of the three among animals producing living young.

These sharks leave the sea, go up the rivers, and there they are no less dangerous than the large alligators, which have already been described in detail, because they too eat men, cows, and horses, and they are very dangerous in the fords and other places where they have feasted.

There are many other species of fish, large and small, that are caught by boats under full sail, and I shall describe the manatee, which is the third of the three fish I said I would describe.

The manatee[95] is a sea fish, much larger than the shark. It is very ugly and resembles those large ox skins used to carry must in Medina del Campo and Arévalo. The head of this fish is as big as a cow's head, and it has eyes like a cow's. It has large stumps instead of arms, with which it swims. It is a very tame animal and comes up to the shore and if there is any grass there that it can reach, it eats it. Since these fish, and many others too, often swim on the surface of the water, they are killed by bowmen in dugouts and boats. When such a fish is sighted, the Indians shoot it with a heavy arrow to which is tied a thin strong cord which has been tarred. Then the fish swims away rapidly and the bowman plays out many yards of the cord, to the end of which is tied a cork or stick. As the fish grows weaker, the sea is covered with blood, and the fish turns toward the shore. The bowman begins to pull in his cord, and when he has pulled in all but a few yards, he draws the cord toward the shore and the manatee finally touches bottom. Then the waves help the fisherman to land the manatee. And the bowman and those who help him drag the manatee up on the shore. A pair of oxen, sometimes two, is required to pull the cart that carries the manatee to the city. Sometimes the fish is loaded into the dugout instead of being towed to shore, because as soon as it dies it floats on the surface. I think that it is one of the tastiest of all fish, and one that tastes most like meat.

It looks so much like a cow that a person seeing only a part that has been cut off could not tell whether it was beef or veal. In fact, it tastes so much like beef that it would fool anyone in the world. It also tastes like the best veal, and it is especially good when dried. None of our fish in Spain, not even the sturgeon, is so good.

The manatee has a certain stone or bone in its head, in the brain or medulla oblongata, which is very useful in curing pain in the side. First the stone is burned, then pulverized. When

95. *Trichechus manatus.*

the pain appears, the patient takes this powder in the morning on an empty stomach. He takes as much as can be picked up on a small coin and follows it with a swallow of good white wine. After continuing this treatment for three or four mornings the pain disappears. Some who have tried the remedy have told me about it. Also I have seen many persons search diligently for this stone for the purpose I have described.

There are other fish almost as large as the manatee that are called red sawfish, which have a sword on the snout. This sword, which is about for or five spans long, is very strong and on both sides it has very sharp teeth. There are other fish that range in size from those smaller than sardines to those so large that two pairs of oxen are necessary to draw them in a cart.

Above I promised to describe other fish that are caught while ships are under sail. Among the many good fish caught in the sea are the tunnies. They are large and good and are caught by throwing gigs or harpoons into them as they swim near the ships. In the same way the dolphin, one of the best, is caught. I have observed one thing about the Atlantic, which can be corroborated by everyone who has made the trip to the Indies. As on land there are fertile as well as barren areas, just so it is at sea. A ship may sail as far as two hundred or more leagues without catching a fish or even seeing one, while in other places of the Atlantic the sea seems to boil with them and many fish are caught.

Now I must speak of flying fish, really a wonderful sight to behold. As ships sail the Atlantic they often encounter many flying fish, the largest being as large or larger than sardines and there are smaller ones. Sometimes they rise in such great numbers that it is a wonder to behold, and again there are only a few. They often fly one hundred paces or more, and frequently they fall in the ships. I remember one night that all on board our ship were kneeling on the after deck singing the *Salve Regina,* when a number of these flying fish rose out of the sea, and many of them fell in our ship. Two or three fell near me, and I held them in my hand and was able to examine them carefully. They were about the size of sardines, and from each side grows a fin as long as the fish, and with these they fly. When these fish rise from the water, they can fly until they become dry. When they dry in the air, they fall again into the water. In 1515, when I first returned to Spain to give your Majesty information regarding the Indies and then went to Flanders in the following year, at the time of your happy accession to the throne of Castile and Aragon, while I was sailing near the island of Bermuda, which is also called la Garza and which is the most distant island known in the world today, I sailed near it until I was in only eight fathoms of water, and about a Lombardy gunshot away. I decided to send a landing party ashore to ascertain the nature of the island and to place there some live pigs, of the stock I had in the ship, to multiply for posterity. But the weather became bad, making it impossible for us to land to possess the island. This island must be about twelve leagues long and six wide and about thirty leagues in circumference. It is north of Santo Domingo at about thirty-three degrees north latitude.

While I was there I saw a great contest between the flying fish, the dolphins, and the sea gulls. I think it was the most interesting sight that could be witnessed on the sea anywhere in the world. The dolphins were swimming at the surface of the water, at times showing their backs, and they would scare up the small flying fish that they were pursuing in order to eat them. The flying fish would rise in the air to escape their pursuers, and the dolphins would dash after them when they fell into the water. At the same time the seagulls would catch many of the flying fish in the air—so that they could find no safety either in the water or in the air. And man experiences this same lack of security in this mortal life, and no one is safe regardless of how high or how lowly his position on earth may be. This alone should be sufficient to cause man to remember the safe abode that has been prepared for those who love Him, to forget his thoughts of the world, so fraught with dangers, and to turn his thoughts to the eternal life which offers everlasting security.

Returning to my history—these birds were of the island of Bermuda, as I have said, and it was near there that I saw this strange sight. Those birds do not go very far from land, and they certainly could not have come from any other place.

## 84

## PEARL FISHING

Since pearls are so much more highly prized than many things I have spoken of, it seems reasonable that I should tell how they are obtained. The Indians and Christians say most of the pearls are found on the North Coast in Cubagua and Cumaná. Many Indians working in groups under leaders, from Santo Domingo or San Juan, leave the island of Cubagua and four, five, or six, or even more go out in a dugout or boat early in the day to where they think they will find a large quantity of pearls. There they anchor the boat, in which one Indian remains, and he keeps the boat as still as he can. The others dive to the bottom. After some time an Indian will return to the surface and deposit in the boat the oysters in which the pearls are found. He rests a while, takes a bite to eat, and once more he enters the water to stay as long as he can, finally returning with more oysters. Meanwhile the other Indians, all good swimmers, are doing likewise. When night falls and they think it is time to rest, they return home to the islands and turn over the oysters to their master's majordomo, who has charge of these Indians. He gives them supper, and puts the oysters in a safe place. When he has many, he has them opened. In each one are found pearls or misshapen pearls, from one to six or more as nature arranged it. They keep the pearls found in the oysters, and eat the oysters if they want them or they are thrown away. There are so many oysters that the excess becomes an annoyance and they are no longer prized as food. These oysters are tough and not as good to eat as ours here in Spain.

This pearl fishing is carried on off the island of Cubagua, off the north coast. This island is about the same size as Zeeland. Sometimes when the sea is rougher than the pearl fisher would like, and also because naturally when a man is working under water at a great depth (as I well know), a diver's feet want to rise, it is only with difficulty that the worker can remain on the bottom any length of time. Under such conditions the Indians use two large stones tied together with a cord, which they place over their shoulders, one on each side, and enter the water. The Indian enters the water and since the stones are heavy, the Indian can remain on the bottom. When he wants to rise to the surface he merely drops the stones. The most marvelous part of this profession is the skill the Indians have for this work, for some of these Indians can remain under the water an hour or more, some less, according to the ability of each one in this endeavor.

Here I am reminded of another important thing. I have asked some of the masters for whom the Indians work if the pearls became exhausted from working such a small spot. They answered that they did, but said that then they would go to fish in another place, and when pearls in that area were exhausted they would go to a new place or return to the first or to other areas previously worked. They remarked that when they returned to a spot that had once been cleaned of all oysters, they found oysters in such abundance that it appeared that none had been taken from the spot. From this one can infer, I suppose, either that the oysters are migratory, as other fish, or that they are produced in very definite places.

Cumaná and Cubagua, the site of the pearl fishing I have described, are at about twelve degrees north latitude off the northern coast of Tierra Firme. Likewise many pearls are found in the South Sea, and larger ones at the Isle of Pearls, which the Indians call Terarequí, which is in the Gulf of San Miguel. There have been found in that place pearls much larger and of far greater value than those found off the North Coast of Cumaná or anywhere else. Here I speak as an eyewitness, for I have been to the South Sea and I have investigated in detail the matter of pearl fishing.

From the island of Terarequí came a pear-shaped pearl that weighed thirty-one carats, which Pedrarias bought for a thousand-odd pesos. He bought the pearl when his cousin Captain Gaspar de Morales went to that island in 1515. Of course that pearl is worth much more than the price paid for it. I also had a perfectly round pearl from that island, as large as a clay pellet shot from a crossbow, which weighed twenty-six carats. In the city of Panama, on the South Sea, I gave six hundred and fifty pesos of good gold for this pearl, and I kept it three years. Since I returned to Spain I sold it to Count Nansao, Marquis of Cenete, your Majesty's great Chamberlain. He gave it to his wife the Marquise of Cenete, Doña Mencía de Mendoza. I think this is one of the largest, perhaps the largest, round pearl ever seen here. On that south coast can be found a hundred large pear-shaped pearls for every large round pearl.

The island of Terarequí, which some Christians call the Isle of Pearls and others of Flores [Flowers], is at eight degrees north latitude off the southern coast of Tierra Firme and in the

*117*

province of Castilla del Oro. Pearls are found in the two places I have mentioned above, that is off both coasts of Tierra Firme. I also have learned that there are pearls in the province and other islands of Cartagena. Since your Majesty is sending me there to be governor and captain, I shall endeavor to find pearls, and I should not be surprised if they should be found there. Those who told me about these pearls got their information from the Indians, who showed them through the lands of Chief Carex, who is the chief of the island of Codego, which is at the mouth of the port of Cartagena, which is called by the Indians Coro. This island and port are at ten degrees north latitude off the northern coast of Tierra Firme.

85

## CONCERNING THE STRAIT AND PASSAGE FROM THE NORTH SEA TO THE SOUTH SEA

It is the opinion of modern cosmographers, pilots, and other experts on the sea that there is a water passage from the South Sea to the North Sea in Tierra Firme. But up to now it has not been discovered. Those of us who know that territory believe the narrows is land, and not a water passage. In certain places the land is so narrow that the Indians say that from the mountains of the province of Esquegna and of Urraca, which lie directly between the two seas, that a man standing on the mountain top there, looking to the north can see the North Sea, at the province of Veragua, and looking to the south can see the South Sea and southern coast of the province of Urraca and Esquegna. If what the Indians say is so, this must certainly be the narrowest part of the land, but since it is said to be so rough, mountainous, and rugged, I do not consider it the best passage or as short as the one from the port Nombre de Dios, on the North Sea, to the new city of Panama, on the South Sea.

This route is difficult to traverse because it is very rough and mountainous and cut by many valleys and rivers. There are also many thick forests. Some say that the distance from sea to sea is eighteen leagues, but I think it is fully twenty and I walked over this route twice in 1521. It is seven or possibly eight leagues from Nombre de Dios to the land of Cacique Juanaga (also called Capira); from there it is a like distance, or further, to the Chagre river, the second day's journey. So to that point I reckon it to be sixteen leagues. That marks the end of the bad road. From there to Puente Admirable it is two leagues and from that bridge it is two more leagues to the Port of Panama. So according to my estimate, the total distance is twenty leagues. Since I have wandered about the world so much and have seen so much of it, it is very easy for me to estimate such a short distance as that between the North Sea and the South Sea.

If there is discovered, as we pray there will be, a water route to the Spice Islands, then the products of those islands can be brought to the Port of Panama and carried over land to the North Sea, in spite of the difficulties I have mentioned above. But there is a very easy way to go to the Spice Islands which I shall describe. From Panama to the Chagre River it is four leagues, covered by a very good road which loaded carts can traverse very easily. Although there are some grades, they are gentle, and for the most of the four leagues the road runs over treeless plains. At the Chagre River the spices could be placed in boats. This river flows into the North Sea five or six leagues below the port of Nombre de Dios. Where it enters the sea there is a small island called Bastimentos, and there it forms a very good port. Just imagine, your Majesty, what a marvelous thing it is for the Chagre River to rise two leagues from the South Sea and then flow to the North Sea. This river has a strong current and is quite wide and deep, all this being well suited to our desires. One could not wish a better arrangement for the purpose I have described.

The following is a description of Admirable or Natural Bridge, which is located two leagues from the above-mentioned river and two leagues from the port of Panama. Going towards Panama, one does not realize the bridge is there until one suddenly comes upon it. From one end of the bridge, looking to the right, a river can be seen below. From where one stands to the water it is about two lance lengths or more in depth. The stream is shallow, about knee-deep, and thirty or forty paces wide. This river flows into the Chagre River, described above. Standing on the bridge and looking to the left there are many trees and the water is not visible. The bridge is about fifteen paces wide and seventy or eighty paces long. By looking underneath where the water flows, it can be seen that it is an arch of living rock, a sight at which any man would marvel, a thing built by the Creator of the universe.

But returning to the matter of the Spice Islands, I say that when our Lord may be pleased to permit us to discover a sea route to that place, and bring its produce to the Port of Panama, to be carried by cart to the Chagre River, from there to the North Sea and then to Spain, more than seven thousand leagues of sailing will be saved. The trip, too, will be much safer than it is now, as your Captain García de Loaísa makes it this year to the Spice Islands. The new route, too, would save two thirds of the time. If those navigating the South Sea had made a diligent effort, I am sure the Spice Islands would have been found some time ago. For I am sure that sooner or later it will be found in the South Sea, according to the opinions of the best cosmographers.

86

## CONCLUSION

Two very notable things can be concluded regarding your Majesty's West Indies in addition to the other details already given, and each one is of the greatest importance. One is the shortness of the route of the South Sea for commerce with the Spice Islands, and the innumerable riches of the provinces and the dominions there, and the different languages and foreign nations. The other is to consider the great treasure that has entered Castile because of these Indies and continues to come in every day, and it is hoped this will continue, gold and pearls and other things that are being brought to your Kingdom every day, things not known or enjoyed by other nations, but only your own subjects. Not only has this nation grown rich, and will grow richer each day, but also surrounding nations have profited immeasurably and beyond description. The best proof of this can be found in your Majesty's double gold ducats, that leave Spain and never return. Since this is the best money that circulates in the world, once it falls into the hands of foreigners it is never released. If it does return to Spain it is in disguise, and is so debased and with your royal insignia so altered that it is hardly recognizable. If this money were not debased in other lands, certainly no Prince could claim such a quantity of good gold as is coined in your Majesty's kingdom. All this wealth comes from the Indies, which I have briefly described above.

\* \* \* \* \*

Sacred, Catholic, Imperial, Royal Majesty: I have written in this short summary or narrative what I have been able to remember of the natural history of the Indies. I have refrained from describing many other things that I do not remember clearly or that I would not know how to describe accurately; nor have I described these things in as much detail as they are to be found in my general and natural history of the Indies, which I have written in my own hand, as I have stated in the prologue of this narrative. This history is in the city of Santo Domingo of the Island Hispaniola.

Most humbly do I beg your Majesty, through your kindness, to accept the good will that moves me to send you this account. Later in greater volume and in more detail you will be able to read all this and everything else I have observed of this sort of thing in the New World. And if your Majesty should be pleased with it, I beg you to have a clear copy made of the longer history so that it may be brought to your royal examination, and then with your permission it may be published. For in truth that history contains things most worthy of being known and held in high veneration. The things described are as true and new to men of this world as anything Ptolemy described in his cosmography. And they are so different and distinct from those described in other histories of this type. For the things in this history are without comparison so strange and unusual that I consider well employed all my night study, as well as the time and labor it has cost me to see and observe these things. And this is especially true if your Majesty should be pleased with such a small service that is offered you by one of the lesser servants of your Sacred, Catholic, Imperial Majesty; your most obedient servant, Gonzalo Fernández de Oviedo, alias de Valdés.

\* \* \* \* \*

The present treatise, entitled *The Natural History of the Indies* by Oviedo, was printed at the expense of the author Gonzalo Fernández de Oviedo, alias de Valdés, through the efforts of Master Remón de Petras, and it was completed in the city of Toledo on the fifteenth day of the month of February in the year 1526.

# GLOSSARY OF PLACE NAMES

Abila=Abyla. In ancient geography, a promontory in Africa, the modern Jebel Musa; opposite the ancient Calpe (modern Gibraltar). The two together constitute the 'Pillars of Hercules' of the ancient geographers.

Abrayme. Province in Castilla del Oro, home of tree-dwelling Indians.

Acla. One of the first towns on the American mainland, in North Panama, on Caribbean side of the Isthmus, near Gulf of San Blas, where Balboa was beheaded; it was founded in 1515 by Pedrarias Dávila; abandoned before 1580.

Andalucía, Andalusia. In general, the south of Spain; specifically the provinces of Almería, Granada, Málaga, Jaén, Córdoba, Sevilla, Cádiz, and Huelva.

Arévalo. Town in Central Spain, province of Avila.

Atrato. River (of Colombia) flowing into the Gulf of Urabá.

Azores. A group of islands belonging to Portugal, in the Atlantic Ocean about 900 miles west of Lisbon.

Bacallao. The Cape Cod area.

Barcelona. City in northeast Spain, important port on the Mediterranean Sea.

Bastimentos. Small island at mouth of Chagres river. Name was later given to port called Bastimento, and also to the anchorage of Bastimentos off Nombre de Dios.

Batibonico=Artibonito (Artibonite). River between Santo Domingo and Haiti; rises in Santo Domingo, flows into Golfe des Gonaïves.

Beata. Island off south coast of Hispaniola.

Boca de Dragón (Dragon's mouth). Strait between the east tip of the peninsula of Paria (Venezuela) and the northwest tip of Trinidad.

Cádiz. Province and city of southeast Spain.

Calpe. Two promontories (Pillars of Hercules) at the eastern end of the Strait of Gibraltar; Calpe (Gibraltar) in Europe and Abyla (Jebel Musa) in Africa. Hercules, it is told, set them there in his search for the Oxen of Geryon.

Canary Islands. Group of islands in Atlantic Ocean off northwest coast of Africa; a province of Spain.

Canoa. Cape north of Cartagena (Colombia).

Caribana. Point (or cape) east side of Gulf of Darién (Colombia).
Cartagena. Part of coast and later city on Gulf of Darién, Colombia.
Castilla del Oro. *See* Tierra Firme.
Catarapa. Province in Castilla del Oro.
Cenú (*also* Sinú). Area between Cartagena and Punta de Caribana; also river flowing into the Gulf of Darién, near Cartagena.
Chagre. Chagres River, Panama.
Codego Island. Mouth of Port of Cartagena.
Colindres. Town in northern Spain, province of Santander.
Coro. Now Cartagena, town on the coast of Venezuela, on the Gulf of Venezuela. *See* Cumaná.
Corobaro. Islands, called by various names, on north coast of Veragua near present Laguna Chiriquí.
Cubagua. Island off coast of Venezuela, west of Trinidad, between Margarita Island and the mainland.
Cueba. Province in Castilla del Oro.
Cumaná. Gulf and City on north coast of Venezuela, west of Trinidad. In 1520 the first European settlement on mainland of South America was established at Cumaná. The colony, not finding gold, migrated further west and founded Coro.
Cutí. River flowing into west side of Gulf of Urabá; also village of Cutí.
Darién. A part of Castilla del Oro. *See* Tierra Firme. (Also Gulf of Darién, in Caribbean Sea between Panama and Colombia, containing the Gulf of Urabá).
Deseada (the desired island), Désirade. One of Lesser Antilles, near Coast of Guadeloupe.
Dominica, La Dominique. One of Lesser Antilles between Guadeloupe and Martinique, so named by Columbus because it first was sighted on Sunday, on the second voyage.
Española (the Spanish Island). Name given to the island by Columbus; later English writers corrupted it to Hispaniola; now Haiti and the Dominican Republic.
Esquegna. Province of the isthmus of Panama, between Veragua and the city of Panama.
Garza. Bermuda.

Gibraltar. *See* Calpe.
Gigantes: Isla de Gigantes (Island of Giants). Curaçao.
Gomera. One of Canary Islands.
Gran Canaria. One of Canary Islands.
Guadalquivir. River of Spain, flowing by Seville and entering the Atlantic Ocean at San Lúcar de Barrameda. This name (and San Juan) originally given to the Atrato River.
Guadalupe, Guadeloupe. One of Lesser Antilles.
Guaturo. Province of Castilla del Oro.
Haina. River of Hispaniola west of Santo Domingo.
Higuey: Cabo de Higuey, Cape Higuey. Cape on east tip of Hispaniola and now called Cabo Engaño.
Hispaniola. *See* Española.
Laredo. Town in northern Spain (in the province of Santander).
Levante, Mar de. Eastern Mediterranean Sea.
Lobos: Cabo de Lobos. Cape on southern tip of Hispaniola.
Marañón. Upper Amazon river, in Peru and Ecuador.
Marigalante, Marie Galante. One of the Lesser Antilles, between the islands Guadeloupe and Dominca, discovered by Columbus in 1493, on his second voyage, and named for his flagship.
Matitino, Martinique. One of Lesser Antilles. The natives called this island by several names: Madiana, Matinina, *etc*. Later it was called Martinico, now corrupted to Martinique. Early maps bear the names Martinino, Matitino, Matanino, and later Martinico, Martinique.
Medina del Campo. Town in north central Spain, province of Valladolid.
Memi, Mennis, *q.v.*
Mennis. Town near ancient city of Babylon. (Quintus Curtius in Book V says that Alexander came to the city of Memi where he found a cave of pitch.)
Middelburg. Capital of the Province of Zeeland, the Netherlands.
Montjuich. Mountain at Barcelona, Spain.
Navidad, La Navidad. Town on North Coast of Haiti, near Cap Haitien, where Columbus built a fort with the remains of his wrecked flagship of first voyage.
New Spain. Mexico.

Nizao. River in the Dominican Republic, which flows into the Caribbean Sea on the south coast, west of Palenque Point.
Nombre de Dios. Town in Panama near the mouth of the Chagres River.
North Sea. The Caribbean Sea.
Ocean Sea. The Atlantic Ocean.
Otoque. Island in Panama Bay.
Ozama. River of Hispaniola that flows into the Caribbean Sea at Santo Domingo (Ciudad Trujillo).
Pánuco. Region near the present Tampico, Mexico, where the Pánuco River empties into the Gulf of Mexico.
Pearl Islands. A group of islands in the Gulf of Panama, the largest being Isla del Rey. It was called Terarequí by the Indians and Núñez de Balboa named it Isla Rica.
Pedernales Mountains. High bluffs on River Pedernales, which flows south into the Caribbean Sea at Anses à Pitre.
Placencia. Town in Northern Spain, province of Guipúzcoa.
Puente Admirable. A natural bridge only a short distance from Panama.
Reiva, Neiba River. River of Hispaniola, also called Yaque del Sur, flows into Bay of Neiba, southern part of island.
Río Grande (Guadalquivir). The Magdalena River, Colombia.
San Blas, Gulf of. Gulf on the North Coast of Panama.
San Cristóbal: the island to which Columbus gave his own name. Irreverently called Saint Kitts by the English. One of Lesser Antilles.
San Juan. River of Colombia that flows into Gulf of Darién, northeast of Gulf of Urabá.
San Juan: Puerto Rico. The name San Juan originally was applied to the whole island as well as to the chief city.
San Juan de la Maguana. A town in the central part of Hispaniola, half way between Santo Domingo and Yaguana, founded in 1503 by Diego Velázquez. No longer in existence.
San Lúcar de Barrameda. City of southwestern Spain, in the province of Cádiz, where the Guadalquivir River flows into the Atlantic Ocean.
San Miguel, Gulf of. A gulf in the Gulf of Panama.
Santa María del Antigua del Darién. One of the first cities in America, built near the mouth of the Atrato river, Colombia; destroyed by the Indians in 1524.

Santa Marta. Town and province, now in Colombia, east of the mouth of the Magdalena River.

Santo Agostín. Name of the easternmost tip of Brazil.

Santo Domingo. City of Hispaniola, long the center of Spanish culture and influence in the New World, now Ciudad Trujillo, Dominican Republic.

Seville. City of southern Spain, location of Board of Trade (India House), which controlled traffic to and from the New World.

Sierra Nevada: Sierra Nevada de Santa Marta. Mountains in Colombia.

Sinú. See Cenú.

South Sea. The Pacific Ocean.

Taboga. Island in Panama Bay.

Terarequí. Largest of the Pearl Islands in the Gulf of Panama. Núñez de Balboa called it Isla Rica; now it is known as Isla del Rey or San Miguel.

Tiburón, Cape. Western tip of Haiti.

Tierra Firme. At the time of discovery this name was given to the entire coast of the mainland south and west of Hispaniola. In 1509 Ferdinand divided Tierra Firme into two parts: Nueva Andalucía, the region extending from the middle of the Gulf of Urabá east to the Cabo de la Vela; and Castilla del Oro, the region extending west from the middle of the Gulf of Urabá to Cape Gracias a Dios. Castilla del Oro was divided into Darién (east), Panama (center), and Veragua (west).

Todos Santos: All Saints. One of the Lesser Antilles, so named because it was discovered on All Saints' Day; named by the French (Iles des Saintes).

Toledo. City and old kingdom of central Spain, once capital of New Castile.

Urabá, Gulf of. Gulf in the Gulf of Darién, in the Caribbean Sea, between the coast of Colombia and Panama.

Valladolid. City and province of central Spain.

Yaguana. Town on west coast of Haiti, destroyed by Osorio in in 1605. Moreau de St. Méry says that it is the present-day Léogane. Haitian historians now believe that it was on the site of the present Port-au-Prince.

Zeeland. Now Island of Welcheren, the Netherlands, part of the Province of Zeeland.

## BIBLIOGRAPHY

### I. Works of Gonzalo Fernández de Oviedo y Valdés
#### HISTORIA NATURAL

*De la natural hystoria de las Indias.* Toledo: Remón de Petras, 1526.

*De la natural historia de las Indias. Historiadores primitivos de las Indias Occidentales.* Ed. Andrés Gonzáles Barcia. Madrid. Tomo I, 1749.

*De la natural historia de las Indias. Historiadores primitivos de Indias;* Ed. Enrique de Vedia, *Biblioteca de Autores Españoles.* Madrid, XXII (1858), 471-515.

*De la natural historia de las Indias. (Sumario de historia natural de las Indias).* Con un estudio preliminar y notas por Enrique Alvarez López. Madrid: Editorial Summa, 1942.

*Sumario de la natural historia de las Indias.* Biblioteca Americana, Serie de Cronistas de Indias. Edición, introducción y notas de José Miranda. Mexico—Buenos Aires: Fondo de Cultura Económica, 1950.

*The Historie of the West Indies.* [Trans.] Eden, Richard. *The Decades of the Newe Worlde or West India.* London: Guilhelmi Powell, 1555. Folios 174-214. ["I have therefore thought good to ioyne to the Decades of Peter Martyr certeyne thynges which I have gathered oute of his [Oviedo's] book intiteled the Sumarie or abbrigement of his generall hystorie of the West Indies." Folio 174r.]

*Of the West Indies. The History of Travayle in the West and East Indies.* Gathered in part and done into English by Richard Eden. London: Richard Iugge, 1577. Folios 185-225.

*Extracts of Gonzalo Ferdinando De Oviedo his Summarie and General Historie of the Indies.* In Samuel Purchas, *Hakluytus Posthumus or Purchas his Pilgrimes.* Hakluyt Society, Extra Series, Glasgow: James MacLehose and Sons, 1906. XV, 148-232. (This had been published originally by Samuel Purchas, London, for Henry Fetherstone, 1625.)

#### HISTORIA GENERAL Y NATURAL

*Primera parte de la historia natural y general de las indias yslas y tierra firme del mar oceano.* Sevilla: [Juan Cromberger], 1535.

*Libro XX. De la segunda parte de la general historia de las Indias.* Valladolid: Francisco Fernández de Córdoba, 1557.

*Historia General y Natural de las Indias, Islas y Tierra Firme del Mar Océano.* Publícala la Real Academia de la Historia. Por D. José Amador de los Ríos. 4 vols. Madrid: Imprenta de la Real Academia de la Historia, 1851-55.

*Historia general y natural de las Indias, Islas y Tierra-Firme del Mar Océano.* Prólogo de J. Natalicio Gonzáles; notas de José Amador de los Ríos. 14 vols. Asunción, del Paraguay: Editorial Guaranía, 1944-45.

\* \* \* \* \*

*Libro de la Camara Real del Príncipe Don Juan e Officios de su casa e servicio ordinario.* Introducción de José Escudero de la Peña. Publícalo La Sociedad de Bibliófilos Españoles, No. 7. Madrid, 1870.

*Las Quinquagenas de la nobleza de España*, publicadas por la Real Academia de la Historia bajo la dirección del académico de número, D. Vicente de la Fuente. Tomo I, Madrid, 1880. [only volume printed]

*Libro del muy esforçado y invencible Caballero de la Fortuna propiamente llamado don Claribalte.* . . . Valencia: Juan Viñao, 1519. [Facsimile edition by the Real Academia Española, Madrid, 1956]

II. OTHER WORKS

Aldrich, John Warren, and Bole, Benjamin Patterson, Jr. *The Birds and Mammals of the Western Slope of the Azuero Peninsula [Republic of Panama].* Scientific Publications of the Cleveland Museum of Natural History. Vol. VII. Cleveland, Ohio, 1937.

Alvarez López, Enrique. "Apuntes acerca de los mamíferos americanos conocidos por Fernández de Oviedo," Associação Portuguesa para o Progresso das Ciências, Tomo V, 4ª Secção, Ciencias Naturais, Congresso de Porto, 1942. Porto: Impresa Portuguesa, 1943, pp. 445-51. [By an editorial error this article was incorrectly attributed to Enrique Fernández López.]

―――. "El 'perro mudo' americano," *Boletín de la Real Sociedad Española de Historia Natural*, XL (1942), 411-17.

―――. "Las plantas de América en la botánica europea del siglo XVI," *Revista de Indias*, VI (April-June, 1945), 221-88.

―――. "Plinio y Fernández de Oviedo," *Anales de Ciencias Naturales*, Madrid, I (1940), 40-61; II (1941), 13-35.

Anderson, C. L. G. *Old Panama and Castilla del Oro.* Washington: The Sudwarth Co., 1911.

Caballero, Arturo. *Flora analítica de España.* Madrid: Sociedad Anónima Española de Traductores y Autores, 1940.

Chardon, Carlos E. *Los naturalistas en la América Latina.* Tomo I, los siglos XVI, XVII, XVIII. Ciudad Trujillo, República Dominicana, 1949.

Cortés, Hernán. *Cartas de relación de la conquista de Méjico.* Buenos Aires: Espasa-Calpe, [1945].

―――. *Five Letters, 1519-1526.* Translated by J. Bayard Morriss, with an introduction. London: G. Routledge & Sons, [1928].

Fernández López, Enrique. *See* Enrique Alvarez López.

Gil Lletget, Augusto. *Sinopsis de las aves de España y portugal.* Trabajos del Instituto de Ciencias Naturales José de Acosta, Serie Biológica. Tomo I, núm. 2. Madrid: Consejo Superior de Investigaciones Científicas, 1945.

Hazard, Samuel. *Santo Domingo, Past and Present; with a Glance at Hayti.* New York: Harper & Brothers, 1873.

Holleman, L. W. J., and Aten, A. *Processing of Cassava and Cassava Products in Rural Industries.* FAO Agricultural Development Paper No. 54. Rome, Italy: Food and Agriculture Organization of the United Nations, March, 1956. [Excellent bibliography pp. 111-15].

Means, Philip Ainsworth. *The Spanish Main, Focus of Envy, 1492-1700.* New York: Charles Scribner's Sons, 1935.

Moscoso, R. M. *Catalogus Florae Domingensis.* Parte I, Spermatophyta. New York: L. and S. Printing Co., 1943.

Murphy, Robert Cushman. *Oceanic Birds of South America.* American Museum of Natural History. New York, 1936.

Rodríguez Demorizi, E. *Relaciones históricas de Santo Domingo.* Ciudad Trujillo: Editora Montalvo, 1942.

Sagarra, J. M. de. *Els Ocells Amics.* Barcelona: Editorial Joventut, 1947.

Santamaría, Francisco J. *Diccionario general de americanismos.* 3 vols. Mexico: Editorial P. Robredo, 1942.

Standley, Paul C. *Flora of Costa Rica.* Field Museum of Natural History, Vol. XVIII, Parts I, II, III, IV. Chicago, 1937-38.

Stejneger, Leonard, and Barbour, Thomas. *A Check List of North American Amphibians and Reptiles.* Cambridge: Harvard University Press, 1933.

Sturgis, Bertha B. *Field Book of Birds of the Panama Canal Zone.* New York: G. P. Putnam's Sons, 1928.

Wilgus, A. Curtis. *The Development of Hispanic America.* New York: Farrar & Rinehart, 1941.

──────. *Histories and Historians of Hispanic America.* New York: The H. W. Wilson Co., 1942.

Wright, Irene A. "The Commencement of the Cane Sugar Industry in America," *American Historical Review,* XXI, No. 4 (July, 1916), 755-80.

# INDEX

Abila, see Abyla.
Abrayme, 40, 41, 93, 123
Abyla, 47, 123
*Accipiter gentilis*, 59
Acedia, 111
Acla, 85, 111, 123
Africa, 47, 49
*Agonostomus monticola*, 110
Aje, 98
*Alcatraz*, 64
Aldrich, John Warren, 130
Alexander the Great, 20, 35
Alligator, 75-78
Almería, 123
Almond, 56
Alphonso of Aragon, xi
Alvarez López, Enrique, vi, 19, 22, 61, 74, 85, 87, 88, 92, 98, 109, 130
Amador de los Ríos, José, 4, 129
Amazon River, 26
Amber, 105
Anacoana, 75
*Ananas sativus*, 99
Andalusia, 79, 84, 123
Anderson, C. L. G., 130
Annatto, 33
*Annona muricata*, 80
Anses à Pitre, 126
Ant, 27, 51, 52, 72, 73
Anteater, 51, 52, 53
Anthill, 51, 52, 53
*Aquila chrysaëtos*, 59
Aragon, 115
*Arbutus unedo*, 88
Areito, 38
Arévalo, 113, 123
Aristotle, vi
Armadillo, 53, 54
Arrow poison, 26, 27, 73, 79, 91
Artibonito River, 8, 123
Asunción (del Paraguay), 4
Aten, A., 131
Atlantic Ocean, xvii, 7, 47, 79, 111, 114
Avila, 123
Avila, Pedrarias de, see Dávila, Pedrarias.
Avocado, 86, 87

Azores, 123

Babylon, 20
*Bacallao*, 35, 123
Badger, 54
Bahama Islands, 28
Balboa, see Núñez de Balboa.
Banana, 100, 101, 102
*Barbacoa*, 29
Barbary, 43
Barbour, Thomas, 131
Barcelona, xiv, 4, 11, 24, 64, 123
Bastimentos, 123
Bat, 46, 62
Batibonico, see Artibonito.
Beads, 44
Bean, 51
Beata (Island), 90, 123
Bee, 72, 73
*Beorí*, 48
Bermuda, 115, 124
*Biajaca*, 110
*Bija*, 33
*Bijao*, 102
Bindweed, 97, 98
Bird, 19, 22, 59, 60
Bird migration, 71
Bird, trapping of, 67
Biscay, 41, 106
*Bixa orellana*, 33
Bloodletting, 43
*Boa constrictor*, 75
Board of Trade, 7
Boca del dragón, 27, 123
*Bohío*, 39
Bole, Benjamin Patterson, Jr., 130
*Boniata*, 17
Booby, 61
*Bothrops atrox*, 74
Brazil, 48
Brittany, 25
Brussels, xiii, 64
Burgos, xv
Burgundy, Duke of, 3
Bushmaster, 74
Bustamante, Diego de, 106

Caballero, Arturo, 130
*Cabra*, 28

*Cabuya*, 42
*Cacique*, 28, 31, 35, 36, 38, 41, 42
Cactus, 99
Cádiz, 47, 123
*Cairina moschata*, 22
Calabash tree, 87
Calleja, Pedro de la, 75
Calpe, 47, 123
*Camayoa*, 105
*Cañafístula*, 9
Canary Islands, xiii, 7, 10, 123
Cancer, 79
Cane, 96
*Caney*, 39
*Canis familiaris*, 57
Cannibalism, 32, 33
*Canoa*, 21, 92, 123
Canoa Point (Cape), 27
Caonabo, 9
Cape Cod, 35
Capira, 118
*Capromys oedium*, 10, 18
*Caranx latus*, 110
*Carduelis carduelis*, 69
Carex, 118
*Cariacus rufinus*, 50
*Cariacus virginianus*, 50
Carib, 33, 44, 57, 60, 79, 91, 106
Caribana Point, 26, 27, 106, 124
Caribbean Sea, ix
*Carica papaya*, 85
Carrot, 98
Cartagena, 27, 33, 56, 57, 92, 106, 118, 124
*Cartas de relación*, 24
Casas, Bartolomé de las, v, xiv, xvii
*Casearia pentandra*, 92
Cassava, 13, 15, 17
*Cassia fistula*, 9, 19
Castile, 58, 66, 97, 114, 120
Castilla del Oro, ix, xiii, xvi, 24, 28, 31, 40, 48, 63, 71, 105, 118, 124
Cat, 11, 49, 70
Catarapa, 43, 124
*Catharista atratus*, 66
Catholic Sovereigns, xi, 3, 4, 89
Cattail, 43
Cattle, 11, 19, 79
*Cavia cobaya*, 10, 18
*Cazabi*, 15
Ceiba, 92

*Ceiba pentandra*, 92
Cenete, Marquis of, 117
Central America, 48, 65
Century plant, 42, 43
Cenú River, 27, 124
Chagre(s) River, 119, 120, 124
Chalcedony, 105
Chancellery, 13
Chaquira, 44
Chardon, Carlos E., 130
Charles V, Emperor, ix, xiii, xiv, xv, xvi, 2, 3, 24, 120, 121
Charles VIII, King of France, 89
*Chelone mydas*, 111
*Chicha*, 39
Chicken, 58, 66
Chickpea, 13
Chigoe, 23
Chili peppers, 41
*Choloepus didactylus*, 54
*Choloepus hoffmanni*, 54
*Chromis fuscomaculatus*, 110
*Chuche*, 51
*Chui*, 32
*Churcha*, 58
Citron, 10, 40
Coal, 109
Coconut, 81, 82, 83
*Cocos nucifera*, 81
Codego, 118, 124
Colindres, 75, 124
Colombia, 126
Colorín, 69
*Columba cyanocephala*, 19
Columbus, Christopher, xi, 4, 24, 47, 48, 49
Columbus, Diego, xiv, xv, 12, 24, 25
*Comején*, 72
Convolvulaceae, 98
*Convolvulus arvensis*, 98
*Copaifera hemitomophylla*, 92
Copper, 19, 35, 110
Córdoba, 123
Corí, 10, 15, 18
Coriander, 97
Cormorant, 59, 65
Corn, 13, 14, 15, 16, 36, 39, 41
Cornelian, 105
Corn wine, 39
Coro, 118, 124
Corobaro, 85, 124

Coronados, 27
Cortés Hernán, 24, 130
Cotton, 9, 29
Cougar, 49, 50
Cow, 11, 79, 112
Crab, 78, 79, 111
Crazy bird, 68
*Crescentia cucurbitifera*, 22
*Crescentia cucurbitina*, 87
*Crescentia cujete*, 87
Crocodile, 77
*Crocodylus acutus*, 76
Cromberger, Juan, xvi, 129
*Crotalidae*, 74
*Crypturus*, 66
Cuba, 7, 17, 19, 20, 21, 24, 25, 42, 50, 83, 111
Cubagua, 116, 117, 124
*Cucumis anguria*, 98
*Cucurbita pepo*, 98
Cueba, 28, 32, 104, 124
Culata, 25
Cumaná, 27, 116, 117, 124
Curaçao, 28, 125
Cutí, 92, 124
*Cyanospiza ciris*, 69
*Cycloturus didactylus*, 51

Dajao, 110
Darién, xiv, xv, 2, 30, 47, 57, 61, 62, 75, 77, 79, 86, 92, 124
Darius, 35
*Danta*, 48
Dávila, Pedrarias, xii, xiii, xiv, xv, xvi, 27, 57, 106, 117
Deer, 15, 29, 50
Deseada (Island), 7, 124
Désirade (Island), 7
Devil, 33, 34, 35, 37
*Dicotyles labiatus*, 50
*Dicotyles tajacu*, 50
*Didelphis aurita*, 58
*Dioscoreaceae*, 98
Dog, 11, 46, 47, 50, 51, 54, 56, 57, 58, 63
Dolphin, 111, 114
Dominica (Island), xiii, 7, 124
Dominican Monastery, 12
Dominican Republic, 4
Domitian, 3
*Don Claribalte*, xiii

*Don Quijote*, xi
Dragon (alligator), 75
Dragon's Mouth, 27
Drumstick tree, 9, 19
Duck, 59, 61
Dugout, 21, 41, 92, 123
Dye, 103

Eagle, 59
*Echeneis*, 21
Ecuador, 125
Eden, Richard, v, 129
Eggplant, 98
*Elaps corallinus*, 59
Emerald, 105
Engaño, Cabo, see Higuey, Cape.
England, 8, 125
Enciso, 62
Enriquillo, Lake, 8
Española, see Hispaniola.
*Espave*, 29
Esquegna, 84, 124
*Estorica*, 26
*Eugerres plumieri*, 110
*Eupsychortyx*, 67

*Falco biarmicus*, 59
*Fanega*, 15
Faro, 3
*Felis concolor*, 49
*Felis onca*, 45, 49
*Felis pardalis*, 49
Fer-de-lance, 74
Ferdinand, King of Naples, 89
Ferdinand, King of Spain, ix, xi, xiii, 3, 4, 27, 48, 60, 78, 89
Fernández de Córdoba, Gonzalo (the Great Captain), xii, 89
Fernández de Oviedo, Gonzalo, v, ix, xi, xv, xvi, xvii, 2, 10, 121, 129
Fernández López, Enrique, 130
Fernández de Valdés, Francisco, xvi
Fire making, 93, 95
Fish, 110
Fishing, 21, 22, 29, 110-15
Fishhook, 56
*Five Letters, 1519-1526*, 24
Flamingo, 59
Flanders, xiii, 25, 40
Flanders, Count of, 3
Flatfish, 111

*135*

Flores, Island of, 117
Fly, 72
Flying fish, 114, 115
Folk songs, 38
Fox, 50
Francis I, King of France, xvi
Franciscan Monastery, 12
*Fregata magnificens*, 60

Gannet, 64
Garza, La (Bermuda), 115, 124
*Gato cerval*, 49
Geese, 22, 23, 59
*General and Natural History of the West Indies*, xvi, xvii, 2, 4, 8, 24, 45, 71, 80, 110
*Genipa americana*, 90
Genipap, 90
Gerfalcon, 59
Germans, 28
Germany, 25
Geryon, Oxen of, 123
Giants, Island of (Curaçao), 28, 125
Gibraltar, Strait of, 24, 25, 47, 125
Gigantes, Isla de, *see* Giants, Island of.
Gilding base metal, 110
Gil Lletget, Augusto, 130
Gold, 19, 36, 106
Goldfinch, 69
Gold mining, 106-10
Gomera, xiii, 7, 125
Gómez, Estéban, 35
Gonaïves, Golfe de, 123
Goshawk, 59
*Gossipium barbadense*, 9
Gourd, 22
Gracias a Dios, Cape, 127
Granada, 123
Gran Canaria, xiv, 7, 125
Grape vine, 85
Great Captain, *see* Fernández de Córdoba, Gonzalo.
Greek, 35, 47
Grijalva, Juan de, xv, 24
Guadalquivir (River in New World), 27
Guadalquivir (River in Spain), 7, 79, 125
Guadalupe, 7, 125
Guadeloupe, 7, 125

*Guaiacum officinale*, 88
*Guaiacum sanctum*, 88
Guajiro, 28
Guarionex, 9
Guaturo, 36, 93, 125
Guava, 81
Guayacan, 88
Guinea, 98
Guipúzcoa, 126
Gull, 59, 61, 115

Haina River, 8, 125
Haiti, 4
Haitien, Cape, 125
Hakluyt Society, v, 129
*Hamaca*, 42
Hammock, 42, 45, 88
Hare, 53
Hawk, 59
Hazard, Samuel, 131
Hazelnut, 97, 98
*Heliconia bihai*, 102
Hemp, 42
*Henequén*, 42, 43
Henry IV, King of Castile, xi
Herbs, 80, 97
Hercules, 47, 48
Hercules, Pillars of, 123
Hernández de Córdoba, Francisco, 24
Heron, 59
*Hico*, 42
Higuera, v, 87
Higuey Point (Cape), 8, 125
*Hippomane mancinella*, 91
Hispaniola, ix, x, xii, xv, xvi, 4, 7, 9, 10, 13, 17, 19, 23, 25, 28, 39, 46, 60, 75, 83, 84, 88, 90, 99, 102, 124, 125
Hog plum, 87, 88
Holleman, L. W. J., 131
Horse, 11, 53, 54, 79
Horsefly, 73
House, Indian, 30, 39-41
Huelva, 123
Humming bird, 70
Hungary, King of, 3
*Huracán*, 37
Hurricane, 37
Hutía, 10, 15, 17
*Hydrobates pelagicus*, 61
Hydrocyanic acid, 18

Iguana, 18, 75
*Iguana tuberculata*, 18
India House, 7, 127
Indian corn, *see* Corn.
*Ipomoea batatas*, 98
*Ira*, 32
Iron, cutting of, 43
Isabella, Queen of Spain, xii, 3, 4, 89
Italy, xvii, 110
Ivy, 98

*Jaba*, 102
Jaén, 123
*Jagua*, 33, 90
Jaguar, 45, 49
Jamaica, 7, 17, 19, 20, 42, 50, 83
Jasper, 105
*Jatropha multifida*, 98
Jebel Musa, 123
Jerusalem, King of, 3
Joanna the Mad, xii
Jobo tree, 87
John, Prince of Aragón, xi, xii
Juanaga, 118
Jurel, 110

Kidney colic, 83
Kite, 60

*Lachesis mutus*, 74
Lanner, 59
La Plata, 69
Laredo, 125
Lemon, 10, 40
Léogane, 127
Leopard, 49
Levant, Sea of, 24, 125
Liana, 39, 40
Lion, 45, 49, 50
Lisbon, 123
Lizard, 18, 53, 75
Loaísa, García de, 120
Lobos, Cape, 8, 125
Lobster, 111
Lucayos, 28
Lynx, 45

*Macana*, 26
Madeira Islands, xiii
Madrid, xii, xiv, 2, 4, 75
Magpie, 69

*Maíz*, 13
Maize, *see* Corn.
Mallard, 59
*Mammea americana*, 80
Mammee, 80
Manatee, 113, 114
Manchineel, 27, 79, 91
*Manihot utillisima*, 16, 17
Manioc, *see* Cassava.
Man-of-war bird, 60
Marañón (Amazon), 26, 125
Margarita (Island), 124
Marie-Galante, 7, 125
Marigalante, 7, 125
Marten, 58
Martinico, 125
Martinique, 7
Matitina, *see* Matinino.
Matitino, 7, 125
Means, Philip Ainsworth, 131
Medina del Campo, 113, 125
Mediterranean Sea, 24, 25, 47, 64
Melon, 98
*Membrillo de montaña*, 86
Memi, *see* Mennis.
Mendoza, Doña Mencía de, 117
Mennis, 20, 125
Merlin, 59
Mexico, 24, 69
Mexico, Gulf of, 126
Middleburg, 105, 125
Miranda José, 68, 92
Mojarra, 110
Monkey, 14, 15, 56, 57
Montjuich Mountain, 12, 125
Morales, Gaspar de, 117
Morris, J. Bayard, 24
Moscoso, R. M., 84, 131
Mosquito, 72
Mullet, 111
Murphy, Robert Cushman, 131
*Musa sapientum*, 100
*Mustela zibellina*, 35
*Myrmecophaga jubata*, 51
*Myrmecophaga tetradactyla*, 51

*Naboría*, 45
Nansao, Count, 117
Naples, 64, 89, 91
*Natural History of the West Indies*, xvi, xvii, 121

*137*

Navidad, 8, 125
Netherlands, 127
New Spain, 24, 63, 105, 125
Neyba River, 8
Nighthawk, 61
Nightingale, 70
*Nigua*, 23
Nizao River, 8, 126
Nombre de Dios, xvi, 118, 126
North Sea, 24, 25, 118, 119, 126
North Star, 30
Nueva Andalucía, 127
Núñez de Balboa, Vasco, ix, xiii, xiv, 41, 62, 123

Oak, 85
Ocean Sea (Atlantic), 24, 25, 61, 126
Ocelot, 49, 50
*Ochi*, 48
Octopus, 111
*Odocoileus virginianus*, 50
*Odontophorus*, 67
*Opistacanthus lepturus*, 78
Opossum, 58
*Opuntia*, 99, 102
Orange, 10, 40
*Oropéndola*, 68
*Ortyx*, 67
Osorio, 127
Otoque, 25, 126
Ovando, Nicolás de, xii
Oviedo, *see* Fernández de Oviedo.
Oviedo, Juan de, xi
Owl, 59
Oyster, 111
Ozama River, 8, 12, 126

Pacific Ocean, 127
*Pájaro bobo*, 61
*Pájaro loco*, 68
Palenque Point, 126
Palm, 82, 83, 84
Palo santo, 88
Panadero, 39
Panama, xiv, xv, 25, 64, 65, 78, 117, 118, 119, 123
Panther, 47
Pánuco (Province and River), 20, 126
Papaya, 85

Paria, 123
Parrot, 14, 60
Partridge, 19, 66, 67
Pasamonte, Miguel de, 12, 109
Pavia, Battle of, xvi
Peacock, 63
Pearl, 118
Pearl fishing, 115-18
Pearls, Island of, 25, 117, 126
*Pecari angulatus*, 50, 51
Peccary, 50
Pedernales Mountains, 126
*Pelecanus occidentalis*, 64
Pelican, 64, 65
Penguin, 61
Pepper grass, 86
*Persea gratissima*, 86
Peru, 125
Petrel, 61
*Pez reverso*, 21
*Phaëton aethereus*, 60
*Phalacrocorax carbo*, 65
*Phalacrocorax graculus*, 65
Pheasant, 67
*Picudo*, 68
*Pinchico*, 69
Pine, 84
Pineapple, 99
*Pintadillo*, 69
*Pinus occidentalis*, 84
Pitch, 20, 27
Pit viper, 27, 73
Placencia, xiii, 126
Plantain, 102
Plants, 80, 97
Pliny, vi, 3, 46, 95, 112
Pompano, 111
Pontano, Giovanni, xii
Porgy, 111
Port-au-Prince, 127
Portugal, 123
Prescott, William, x
Prickly pear, 102
*Procyon cancrivorus*, 56
*Psidium guayaba*, 81
Ptolemy, 8, 47
Puente Admirable, 119, 120
Puerto Rico, *see* San Juan (Puerto Rico).
Purchas, Samuel, v, 129
Purgatives, 97, 98

Purslane, 97

Quail, 59
*Quercus*, 85
*Quevi*, 28
Quince, 86
Quintus Curtius, 20
*Quiscalus macrourus*, 68

Rabbit, 18, 53, 54, 58
Raccoon, 56
Raleigh, Sir Walter, x
Rao, Francisco, 75
Rat, 58
Ray, 110
Reiva River, 126
*Remora*, 21, 22
Rey: Isla del Rey, 127
*Rhynchotus*, 66
Rica: Isla Rica, 127
Ring dove, 59
Río Grande, 126
Ríos, Pedro de los, xvi
Rodríguez Demorizi, E., 131
Roman, 35
Romances of Chivalry, xi
Royal Council of the Indies, xv, 2, 34, 40
*Roystonea regia*, 84

*Sabana*, 107
Sable, 35
*Saco*, 28
Sagarra, J. M. de, 131
Saint Bartholomew, 37
Saintes, Iles des, 7
Saint Francis, Monastery of, 12
Saint John's day, 31
Saint Kitts, 7, 126
Saint Mary of Mercy Monastery, 12
St. Méry, Moreau de, 127
Saint Michael the Archangel, 37
San Blas, Gulf of, 123, 126
San Cristóbal, 7, 126
San Juan (Puerto Rico), xiv, 7, 17, 19, 50, 62, 83, 116, 126
San Juan de la Maguana, 8, 126
San Lúcar de Barrameda, xii, xv, 7, 8, 79, 126
San Miguel, Gulf of, 117, 126
Sannazaro, Jacopo, xii

San Román, 93
Santamaría, Francisco J., 131
Santa María del Antigua, xiii, xiv, xv, xvi, 2, 30, 47, 71, 92, 126
Santa Marta, xiii, 27, 50, 77, 105, 127
Santander, 125
Santiago, Cuba, xv
Santo Agostín, 30, 127
Santo Domingo, ix, xiii, xv, xvi, xvii, 4, 7, 8, 11, 13, 19, 50, 83, 85, 90, 115, 116, 121, 127
Sapphire, 105
*Sarcopsylla penetrans*, 23
Sardine, 64, 65, 66, 110, 114
Sawfish, 114
Scorpion, 27, 77
Serpent, 74
*Serranus inermis*, 110
Sevilla, xiii, xvi, 4, 7, 47, 123, 127
Shad, 21, 111
Shark, 111-13
Shrimp, 110
Sicily, xvii, 3, 9, 91
Sierra Nevada, 27, 127
Silver, 35
Sinú, *see* Cenú.
Sisal hemp, 42
Skull, thickness of, 43
Sloth, 54, 55
Snake, 74
Sodomy, 104, 105
*Soldadito*, 69
Soursop, 80
South Sea, 24, 25, 117, 118, 119, 120, 127
Spain, xv, 4, 7, 8, 10, 25, 30, 31, 32, 47, 50, 54, 56, 61, 66, 85, 95, 97, 110, 114, 117
Spice Islands, 119, 120
Spider, 78
*Spondias lutea*, 87
Standley, Paul C., 131
Stejneger, Leonard, 131
Stock dove, 59
Strawberry tree, 88
Sturgis, Bertha B., 131
Sugar, 10, 19
Suicide, 35-37
*Sula bassana*, 64
*Sula fusca*, 61

*139*

Sumario, 4
Swallow, 59
Sweet potato, 41
Swift, 61
Swine, 15, 16, 29, 50
*Symphurus plagusia,* 111
Syphilis, 18, 88, 89

Taboga, Island of, 25, 127
Tampico, 126
*Tanagra bonaerensis,* 69
Tapir, 48, 49
*Tapirella bairdi,* 48
*Tapirella dowi,* 48
*Tapirus terrestris,* 48
*Tatusia novemcincta,* 53
*Tayassus pecary,* 50
Tequina, 33, 34, 35, 39
Terarequí, 25, 117, 127
Termite, 72, 73
Thrush, 61, 69
*Tiburón,* 111
Tiburón, Cape, 8, 127
Tick, 104
Ticknor, George, x
Tide, 24-26, 64
Tierra Firme, ix, xii, xiii, 3, 7, 8, 9, 13, 15, 17, 19, 21, 23, 24, 25, 28, 35, 39, 45, 46, 48, 50, 54, 56, 58, 62, 67, 71, 79, 80, 84, 88, 91, 96, 103, 105, 117, 118, 127
Tiger, 45-48, 50
Tigris River, 45
*Tinamus,* 66
*Tiva,* 28
Toad, 79
Todos Santos, 7, 127
Toledo, ix, 16, 35, 45, 48, 65, 93, 127
Torrid Zone, 29, 30
Toucan, 68
*Trachinotus galucus,* 111
*Trachinotus ovatus,* 111
Tree, 80, 92, 93
*Trichechus manatus,* 113, 114
Trinidad, 123
Trojan, 35
Tropic bird, 60
Tropic of Cancer, 29
Tropic of Capricorn, 29

Trout, 110
Trujillo, Ciudad, 127
*Tuna,* 102
Turkey, 63, 64, 66
Turtle, 21, 22, 111
Turtle dove, 19
*Tuyra,* 34
*Tyassus pecari,* 50

Urabá, Gulf of, xiii, 25, 26, 30, 41, 91, 127
*Urocyon cinereoargentatus,* 50
*Urocyon virginianus,* 50
Urraca, 84

Valencia, xiii
Valladolid, xvii, 105, 127
Vela, Cabo de la, 127
Velázquez, Diego, xv, 24, 126
Venezuela, 124
Venezuela, Gulf of, 124
Veragua, 85, 127
Vergara, Margarita de, xii
Vermin, 104
Vespatian, 3
Villacastur, Francisco de, 57
Villahermosa, Duke of, xi
Viper, 27, 73
*Vitis quinquefolia,* 85
Vitoria, ix, xv
*Vulpes virginianus,* 50
Vulture, black, 66

Wasp, 72
Welcheren (Island), 127
Wilgus, A. Curtis, 131
Winged ants, 73
Wolf, 57
Wright, Irene A., 131

Y, 97
Yaguana, 8, 19, 127
Yam, 17, 98
Yáñez Pinzón, Vicente, 26
Yuca, 15, 16, 17, 41, 46
Yucatan, xv, 105
Yuste, xvii

*Zea mays,* 13
Zeeland, 105, 116, 127
Zopilote, 66

The Department of Romance Studies Digital Arts and Collaboration Lab at the University of North Carolina at Chapel Hill is proud to support the digitization of the North Carolina Studies in the Romance Languages and Literatures series.

DEPARTMENT OF
**Romance Studies**
Digital Arts and Collaboration Lab

www.ingramcontent.com/pod-product-compliance
Lightning Source LLC
Chambersburg PA
CBHW020417230426
43663CB00007BA/1207